Heidi Zuckerman [HZ.2005]

PAGE 4

TYPE Essay

TITLE *Pay Attention Mother Fuckers*

AAM HISTORY Heidi Zuckerman is the Nancy and Bob Magoon CEO and Director of the Aspen Art Museum, appointed in 2005. To date at the AAM, she has curated over seventy-five exhibitions, including traveling exhibitions to over fifteen venues across North America. She also established the Aspen Art Press, which has produced over forty exhibition catalogues distributed nationally and internationally. For this issue, Zuckerman has chosen to reprint an essay from her 2008 group exhibition, *Now You See It.*

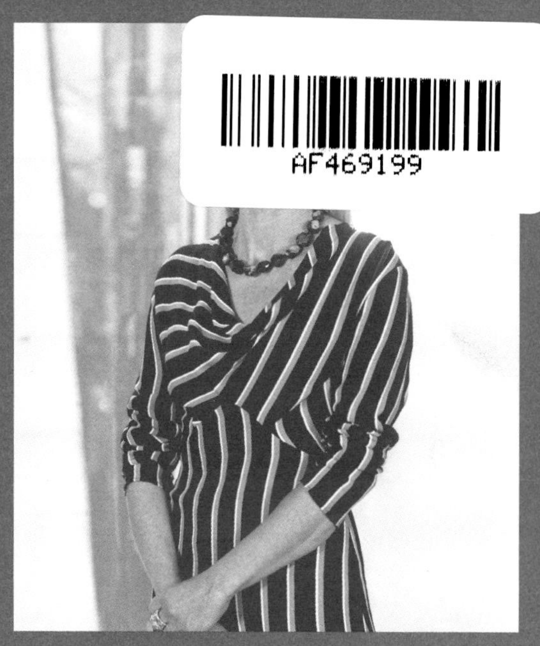

Photo: Karl Wolfgang

Douglas Fogle [DF.2011]

PAGE 16

TYPE Essay

TITLE *On the Road with Catherine Opie*

AAM HISTORY Douglas Fogle is an independent curator and writer based in Los Angeles. His contribution to this issue is a reflection on Catherine Opie's artistic practice, outlining its humanistic, dignified nature. Fogle first collaborated with the AAM to curate Mark Manders's *Parallel Occurences/Documented Assignments*, a 2011 exhibition coorganized with the Hammer Museum in Los Angeles where he was Chief Curator and Deputy Director at the time.

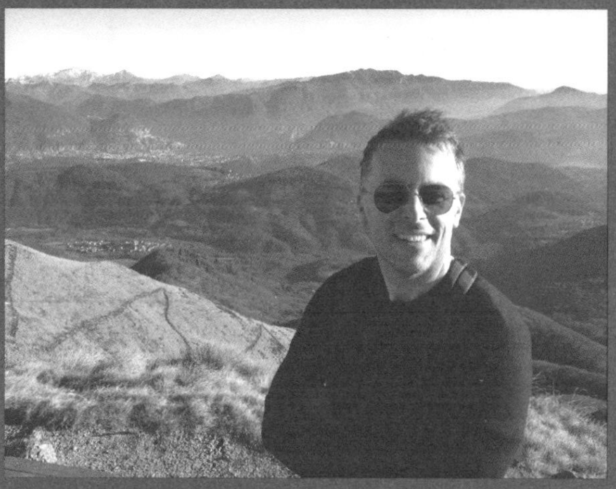

Courtesy Douglas Fogle

Catherine Opie [CO.2010]

PAGE 16; 20

TYPE Essay (Douglas Fogle); Images

TITLE *On the Road with Catherine Opie; Surfers* Series

AAM HISTORY Catherine Opie, a Los Angeles–based artist primarily working in photography, largely focuses on marginalized communities in America through portraiture. She is invested in documenting cultural identity as well as social and gender codes and their inability to be physically understood. Douglas Fogle's text on Opie's practice is followed by a selection of images from her *Surfers* series, depicting surfers amid dreamy, distant Malibu seascapes. Opie first donated to ArtCrush in 2010, and more recently, her work was included in the 2015 group exhibition *The Blue of Distance*.

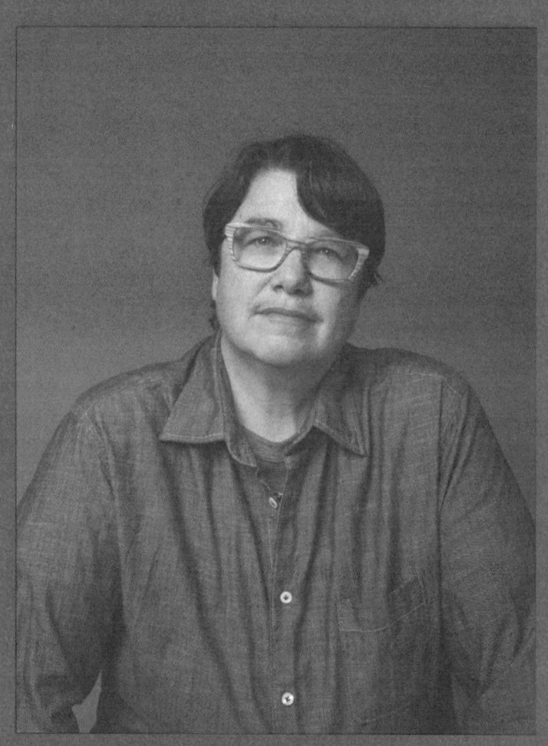

Photo: Heather Rasmussen. Courtesy the artist and Regen Projects, Los Angeles

David Foster Wallace [DFW.2018]

PAGE 26

TYPE Speech

TITLE *This is Water*

AAM HISTORY For this issue, the AAM reprinted literary author David Foster Wallace's (1962–2008) famous commencement address presented to students of Kenyon College in 2005. Full of humor and agony, the speech poses challenging but relatable questions for everyone, regardless of age or experience. This is the first time Wallace's writing has been included in an AAM publication.

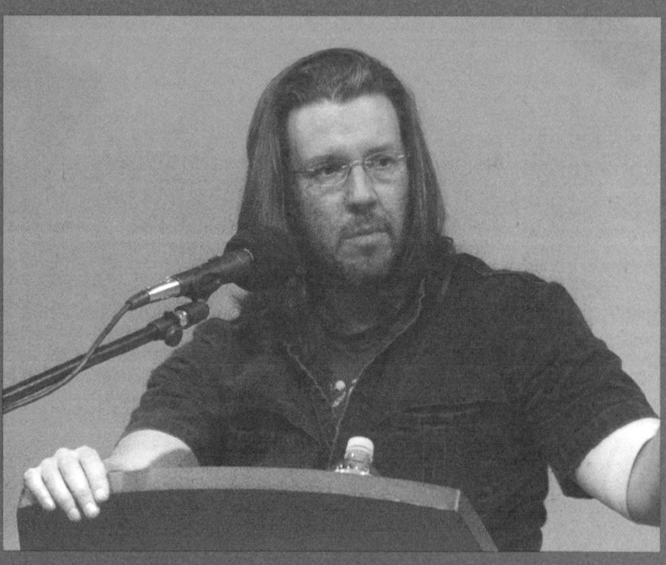

Photo: Steve Rhodes

George Baker

[GB.2018]

PAGE 32

TYPE Essay

TITLE *Paul Thek: Notes from the Underground*

AAM HISTORY George Baker is currently Professor of Art History at the University of California Los Angeles, where he has taught since 2003. Baker's contribution, originally published in Paul Thek's 2010 retrospective exhibition catalogue, is an excerpt from his essay on Thek's newspaper paintings that, as he argues, communicate an "oceanic" feeling of depth, often through the representation of swimmer's bodies. This is Baker's first collaboration with the museum.

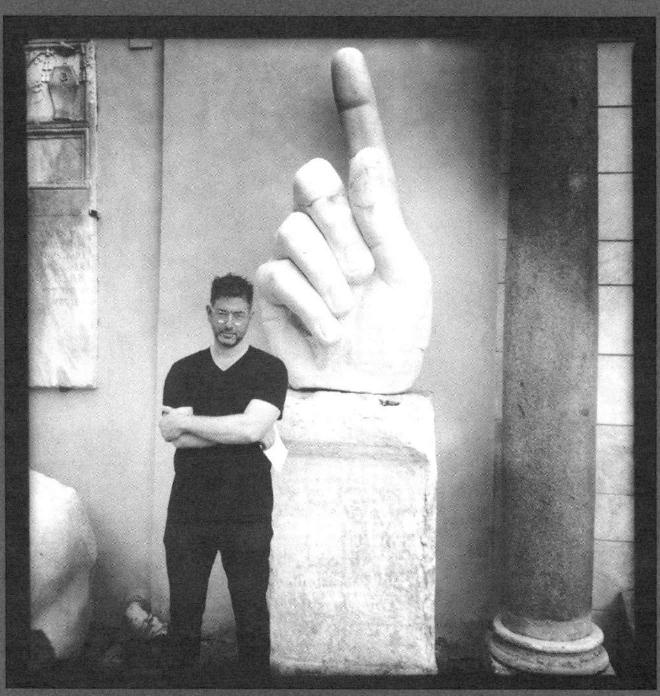

Courtesy George Baker. Photo: Silvia DiPierdomenico

Paul Thek

[PT.2018]

PAGE 32

TYPE Essay (George Baker)

TITLE *Paul Thek: Notes from the Underground*

AAM HISTORY Paul Thek (1933–1988) was a New York–based painter known for his performative sculpture and room-size installations made of banal, recycled materials. Thek's newspaper paintings—compositions that incorporate collected moments in time, conveying a vulnerability and sense of melancholy—are the subject of the text by George Baker in this issue. This is the first time that the artist's work has been featured at the AAM.

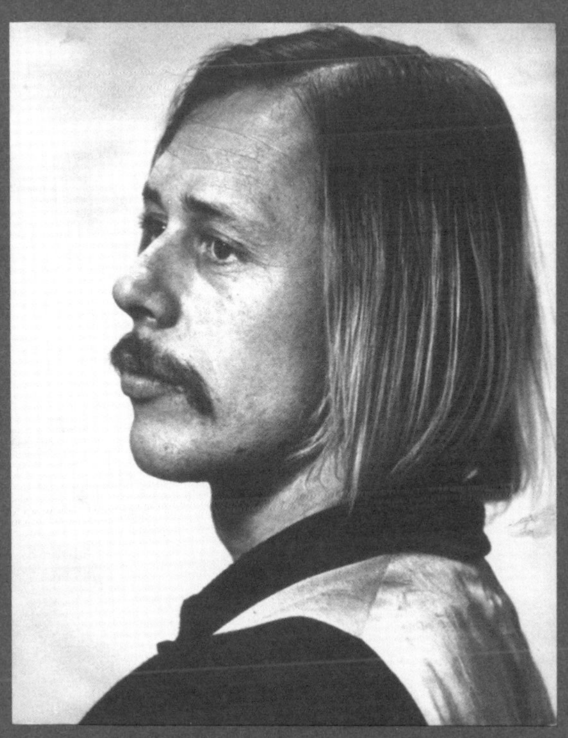

Paul Thek, ca. 1967. Courtesy Alexander and Bonin, New York. Photo: Aimee Rhum

Sol LeWitt [SL.1995]

PAGE 38

TYPE Correspondence

TITLE Letter to Eva Hesse, April 14, 1965

AAM HISTORY Sol LeWitt (1928–2007) was a pioneer of conceptual art who redefined what art could be. He determined that directions for executing his ideas were the work of art itself—these pieces often exist only on paper, as strict instructions for others to pursue. This issue includes the artist's correspondence with Eva Hesse, who was a close friend and, as can be seen in his advice on the following pages, a confidant. LeWitt's *Wall Drawing #159* was featured in the AAM exhibition *Contemporary Drawing: Exploring the Territory* in 1995.

Eva Hesse [EH.2016]

PAGE 38

TYPE Correspondence (Sol LeWitt)

TITLE Letter to Eva Hesse, April 14, 1965

AAM HISTORY Eva Hesse (1936–1970) was a German-born American artist best known for her abstract, Post-Minimalist sculpture. With a deep psychology and vulnerability of the human body always central to her practice, her metaphorical works have been said to evoke a raw femininity. This is the Aspen Art Museum's second time featuring Hesse's work, which was on view during the screening of her 2016 documentary directed by Marcie Begleiter.

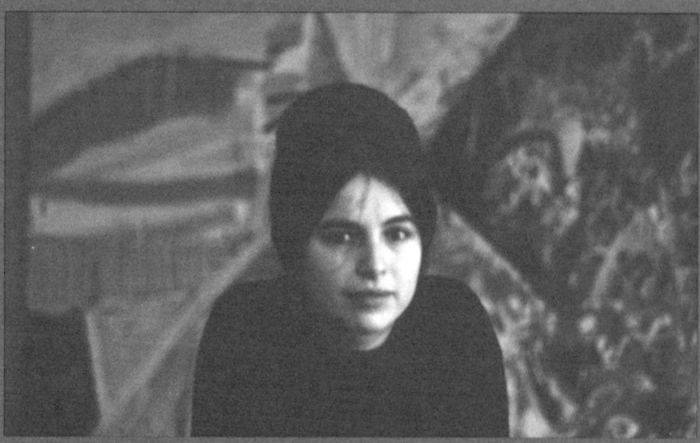

Eva Hesse in her loft, Lower Manhattan, 1963. © The Estate of Eva Hesse. Courtesy Hauser & Wirth. Photo: Barbara Brown

Isa Genzken [IG.2017]

PAGE 44

TYPE Exercise Notes

TITLE *Two Exercises*

AAM HISTORY Isa Genzken is a German artist working in a variety of media and living in Berlin. Largely influenced by architecture, her practice was initially associated with sleek Minimalism in the nineties, but shifted toward a radical approach to assemblage. Genzken was greatly influenced by fellow artist Bruce Nauman while a student at the Düsseldorf Art Academy, and her reflection included in this issue is a response to his instructive body and mental exercises created the same year. Genzken's first time working with the AAM was in 2017 for the group exhibition *Gravity & Grace*.

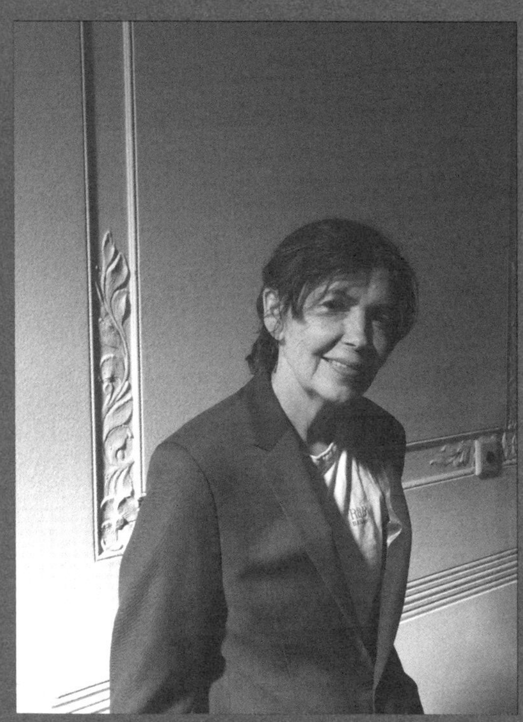

Isa Genzken, 2015. Courtesy Galerie Buchholz, Cologne/Berlin/New York

Bruce Nauman [BN.1979]

PAGE 46; 48

TYPE Exercise Notes; Drawings

TITLE *Instructions (for a mental exercise)*

AAM HISTORY Widely regarded as one of the most important conceptual artists, Bruce Nauman is invested in exploring the body as a medium, word play, and language and communication through a wide range of media. Nauman first worked with the museum in 1979—when it was known as the Aspen Center for the Visual Arts—for the show *American Portraits of the Sixties and Seventies*. His contribution to this issue is a reprint of his *Instructions (for a mental exercise)*, first published in *Interfunktionen* in 1974. The text and accompanying images propose exercises that Isa Genzken responds to in her contribution—which was also originally featured in the same publication. A similar set of Nauman's exercise instructions will be included in the forthcoming 2018–19 exhibition *Lost Without Your Rhythm*.

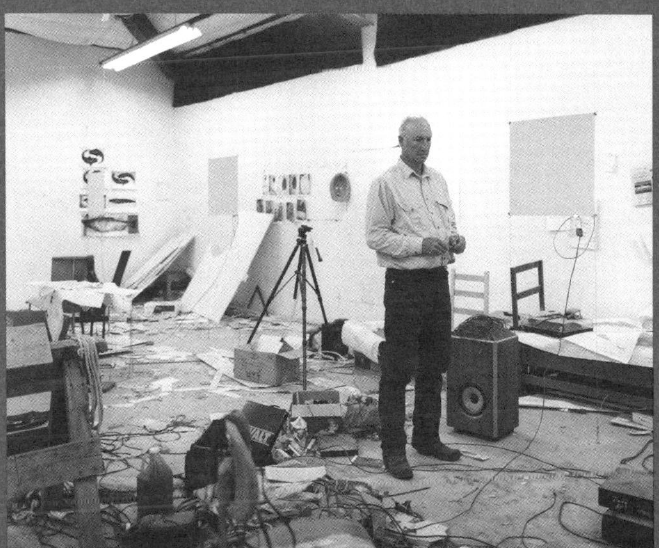

© 2017 Bruce Nauman / Artists Rights Society (ARS). Courtesy Sperone Westwater, New York. Photo: Jason Schmidt

Hélio Oiticica [HO.2018]

PAGE 52

TYPE Cinema Experiment Notes

TITLE *Nitro Benzol & Black Linoleum*

AAM HISTORY Within this issue is one of the first screenplays created by the late Brazilian artist Hélio Oiticica (1937–1980), conceived in 1969—what he would later call his hybrid Quasi-cinemas. Incorporating installation with film and sound, the pieces merge participating artists with the audience, resulting in improvised actions to create surreal, immersive environments. This is the first instance Oiticica's work has been included in an AAM program.

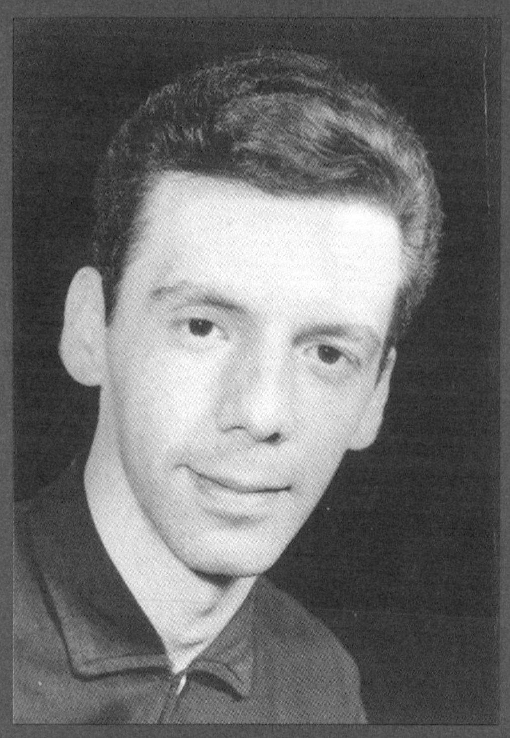

Courtesy the artist

Lynda Benglis [LB.2016]

PAGE 58

TYPE Interview

TITLE *You Can't Change Anything*

AAM HISTORY Lynda Benglis is a sculptor living and working in Taos, New York, and Ahmedabad, India. She first gained visibility for her latex "spills" in the late sixties that offer tactile extensions of the body, and later, her video works that continued to explore physicality and identity while exposing the limitations of the medium itself. Benglis previously worked with the AAM on her 2016 Roof Deck Sculpture Garden installation of vibrant pink fountains—forms that she has been working with for decades.

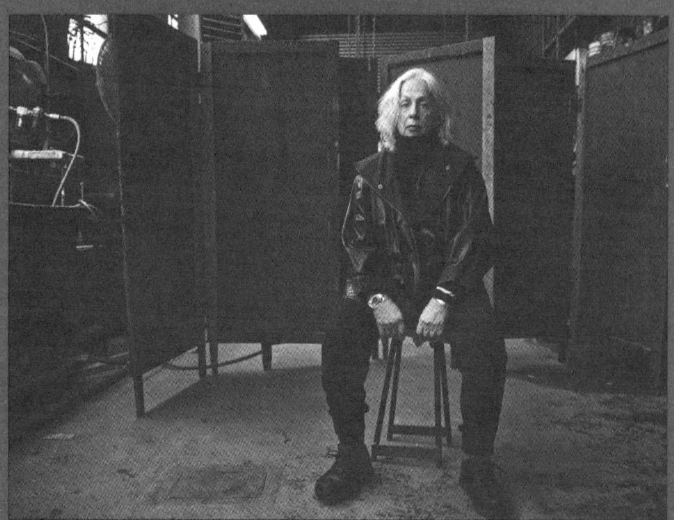

Portrait of Lynda Benglis at Modern Art Foundry. Photo: Sebastian Kim

Paul Chan

[PC.2006]

PAGE 66

TYPE Visual Essay

TITLE *Variation on 1.066*

AAM HISTORY Paul Chan is an artist and writer living and working in New York. He is the founder of the publishing house Badlands Unlimited. Within his practice, he is invested in challenging the possibilities for making and experiencing the moving image, while also blurring the difference between imagination and reality, and visibility and invisibility. Chan first collaborated with the AAM in 2006 for the group exhibition *Belief and Doubt.*

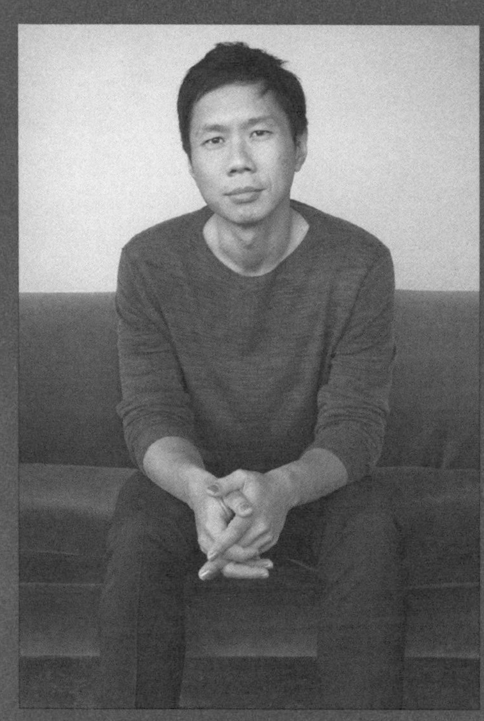

Courtesy the artist. Photo: Eric Boman

Jay Heikes

[JH.2011]

PAGE 72

TYPE Essay

TITLE *Winter is Not Coming.*

AAM HISTORY Jay Heikes is a Minneapolis-based artist working in a variety of media to construct objects that fall somewhere between installation, sculpture, painting, and drawing, focusing on alchemy, science, and transformation through natural decay. His objects possess a sense of wonder and are the result of comingling numerous dissimilar materials. Heikes first worked with the AAM for ArtCrush in 2011, and following that, his work *Buried in the Bright* was part of the museum's New Site Commissions in 2012.

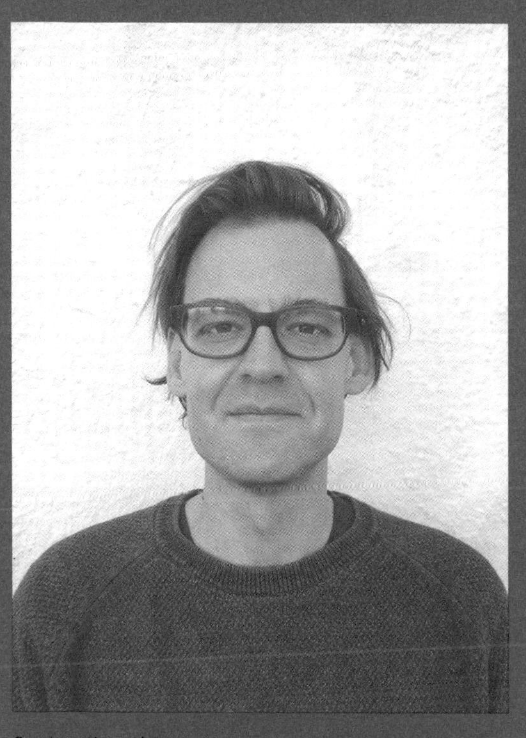

Courtesy the artist

J.G. Ballard

[JGB.2018]

PAGE 84

TYPE Short Story

TITLE *Dream Cargoes*

AAM HISTORY J.G. Ballard (1930–2009) was a British author and key figure in the New Wave movement in science-fiction writing. He composed numerous surreal novels with apocalyptic tones exploring dystopian modernity, including *The Atrocity Exhibition*, *Crash*, *Concrete Island*, and *Empire of the Sun*. His short story "Dream Cargoes" from 1990 is featured in this issue, marking Ballard's first connection with the museum.

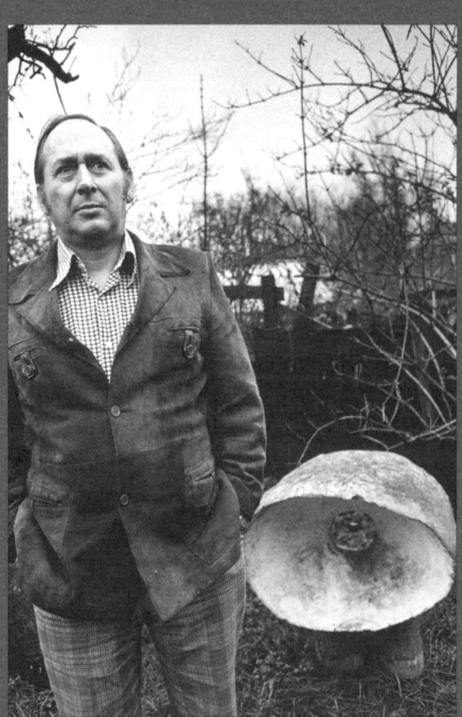

J.G. Ballard. Courtesy the British Library. Image: Fay Godwin

Renée Green

[RG.2018]

PAGE 96

TYPE Essay

TITLE *Now It Seems Like A Dream*

AAM HISTORY Renée Green is a multimedia installation artist, filmmaker, and writer based in New York and Cambridge, MA, where she is Professor in the Art, Culture, and Technology program at Massachusetts Institute of Technology. Her practice investigates public and private memory and the imagined and invented. Furthermore, Green's work explores how people relate to built structures and locations that are only temporarily inhabited, which is evident in her text *Now It Seems Like A Dream*, published in her recent book, *Other Planes of There: Selected Writings*. This is Green's first occasion working with the AAM.

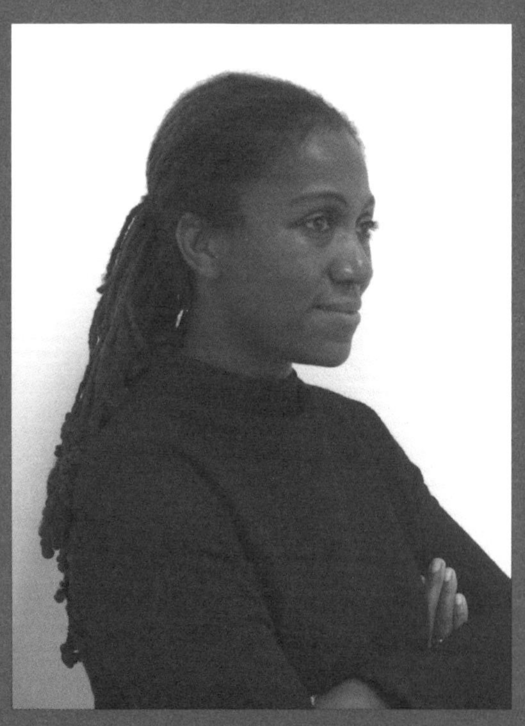

Courtesy the artist

Director's Foreword

Permanent Collection mines our archives as well as our minds to offer ideas about how we are thinking about the making and experiencing of art. As you know, we believe that artists, curators, and writers help define culture, and together, we celebrate its transformative power. In this issue, we specifically focus on meaning and "being": the space in consciousness between stillness and action, informing and preceding any act of "doing." A pause in this innate state, through heightened awareness, can connect to a magical, enlightening possibility.

The title of this issue, "it came to feel like any other feeling," comes from Paul Chan's contribution. This idea, while at first potentially comforting, creates an echo suggesting that consistency can also breed complacency, and consequentially, inertia. Our idea of "-ing" is one of presentness, mindfulness, and conscious decision-making.

Being comes to the fore in my opening essay on the 2008 AAM group exhibition *Now You See It*. The title, "Pay Attention Mother Fuckers," is drawn from Bruce Nauman's 1973 text-based print that serves as both a mantra and directive for awareness. Exploring notions of transformation, the consciousness and materiality of objects, and the primacy of the act of seeing, I emphasize the powers of observation that enable all consequential interactions with visual art.

Douglas Fogle's essay, "On the Road with Catherine Opie," argues that Opie's photographic formalism is intensely concerned with what it means to be a part of the American community. The artist's *Domestic*, *Freeway*, and *Mini-malls* series as well as her book *East, Middle, West* (2000) offer observations on the complexity of the nation. By highlighting the many ways of being American, the artist puts forth "a mosaic" of compelling, singular images rather than an improbably cohesive whole.

Paying attention is also at the center of David Foster Wallace's timeless 2005 commencement speech at Kenyon College. "This is Water" begins with a simple, yet resonant parable, revealing that "the most obvious, ubiquitous, important realities are often the ones that are the hardest to see and talk about." Yet, Wallace believes it is within our power to seek out what is "hidden in plain sight." By so doing, we can consciously construct an outlook that not only improves our most ordinary and even frustrating experiences, but also heightens our powers of empathy.

Also taking their cue from the essential, meditative nature of water are Paul Thek's newspaper paintings, the focus of George Baker's essay "Paul Thek: Notes from the Underground." Thek's series, begun in 1969, superimposes painterly meditations over the most ordinary of surfaces, prioritizing personal, lived experience over our culture's often unremitting, distracting flow of information. The artist's serene pools of water punctuated by solitary swimmers as well as works like *Periscope* (1979–80) and *Diving Swan* (1975) serve as a "testament to art's immense depths" and the power of contemplative being.

Accessing the transformative potential of art and creativity often requires emptying the mind of distraction through doing. This is exactly what Sol LeWitt advocates in his letter to Eva Hesse (from April 14, 1965). For LeWitt, overthinking or wrong thinking foments self-doubt and estrangement from intuition. LeWitt instead encourages Hesse to bravely practice such universal fears as "being stupid, dumb, [and] unthinking" in order to more freely and confidently create. Also drilling consciousness through action is Isa Genzken's "Two Exercises." By putting her body through the performance of repeated actions, as delineated by Bruce Nauman, and taking time to observe and describe the progression of her mental and physical being, Genzken illustrates an increasing mastery over her own experience.

Nitro Benzol & Black Linoleum, one of Hélio Oiticica's first screenplays or Quasi-cinemas, was conceived by the artist in London in 1969. In this work, Oiticica upends the traditional formula for passive audience reception. Watching is replaced with roughly scripted, improvised actions and immersive environments that ask people to see, feel, taste, smell, and participate, thereby activating the imaginative power of the viewer.

My conversation with artist Lynda Benglis on the occasion of her 2016 solo exhibition at the AAM similarly endorses audience participation. In our discussion of her artistic practice, Benglis's philosophy is front and center: all art is rightly subject to individual interpretation. In fact, according to the artist, you should "read anything you want into it."

Paul Chan's "Variation on 1.066" introduces the works in this issue that explore imagining and dreaming. Blurring fiction and reality, Chan offers topical, dreamlike thoughts on universal experiences such as storytelling, living, and dying, often presented through the perspective of familiar celebrity characters like Charles Barkley and Joan Rivers. Paired with images constructed from everyday digital symbols, Chan's text makes visible the layered and often hidden meanings that underlie human thinking and communication.

In his essay "Winter is Not Coming," artist Jay Heikes tells the personal story of Pier Paolo Calzolari's impact on his life and work, describing the artist's practice as a "utopian living theater." For Heikes, Calzolari's oeuvre is a poetic testament to the primacy of dreams and observation, inspiring a wonderment of life's essence. Calzolari's profound symbols "bring thought to form" and find meaning in the banality of the everyday.

We are reminded of the importance of protecting and cherishing our interior lives in science-fiction writer J.G. Ballard's "Dream Cargoes" (1990).

In this story, a young sailor named Johnson is grounded on an island while his barge spills hazardous organic waste. This leak results in brilliant, fantastical new life forms and seems to initiate new planes of consciousness for Johnson.

We conclude with Renée Green's "Now It Seems Like a Dream," from her book *Other Planes of There: Selected Writings* (2014). This text highlights the fleeting experiences of contemporary life as well as their lingering memory. She asks how we make sense of and find value in the succession of places we encounter and our many sensorial and cognitive observations. A sustained reckoning with this question is ultimately the essence of living.

Thank you in advance for spending some time with what we have assembled here. I think you will be grateful you took the time and made the space to do so!

—Heidi Zuckerman
Nancy and Bob Magoon CEO and Director

Heidi Zuckerman

Pay Attention Mother Fuckers

"I once was lost, but now am found, Was blind, but now I see."
—John Newton, "Amazing Grace" (1779)

At their best, people and works of art allow a reprieve from the blindness with which we traditionally see our world. When the white blindness that afflicts all of the characters except for the doctor's wife in José Saramago's novel *Blindness* finally abates, she reasons, "Why did we become blind, I don't know, perhaps one day we'll find out, Do you want me to tell you what I think...I don't think we did go blind, I think we are blind, Blind but seeing, Blind people who can see, but do not see."[1] What is the root cause of the blindness in Saramago's book? For his characters, it is endemic. It affects all but one of them. The one who can see is left to witness the acts of the others. Unbeknownst to them, she becomes not only their sight, but also the recorder of their actions, the consciousness of the collective. Literary scholars have suggested that the blindness is, in fact, a pathology or a failure of consciousness. Saramago illustrates how quickly society breaks down when the ability to see beyond the tangible vanishes and hope abates. The metaphor resonates today, asking why—and what—can we not see?

Ad Reinhardt said, "The boundaries of seeing, like the perceptible aspects of nature or outer space, seem to extend as indefinitely as man's experience and experiments can take them. Art teaches people how to see."[2] Reinhardt's *Black Paintings* seem, at first, to be vast fields of pure blackness. Their apparent absence of pictorial interest challenges dismissive assumptions by traditional art viewers. If, however, they look harder and longer, then they might feel compelled and find subtle grids or shades of color.[3] Peering deep into the frame, allowing oneself to be comfortable with the blackness, facilitates a glimpse into the dark depths of one's soul and access to the space of fear, unknowing, and death. The *Black Paintings* offer perspective on the longevity of vision, commitment to seeing, and an opportunity to transcend the immediate. They reward the persistent. Their magnificence is, however, often overlooked by viewers too quick, skeptical, or blind to see.

That Reinhardt's paintings—absent of imagery—are elevated to the status of art can also arouse suspicion. From the adoption of the readymade by Marcel Duchamp to contemporary performances by Tino Sehgal, it is understandable that many people feel as if they are being duped as claims of transcendence are made for these relatively unassuming acts. Walter Benjamin wrote about the "aura" of works of art, how they can be imbued with an animate energy. The embodied magic of the artworks included in *Now You See It* counters the condition of blindness. When something stops being what it was before—dust, string, felt, even looking—and becomes something else, becomes art, a fissure forms.

Now You See It draws upon unconventional notions of transformation—like alchemy and magic—as a way of understanding this process as more than simply an elevation of base materials. As viewers, we hope for magic, against its impossibility. Yet, of course, it occurs. We know that human perception is a jerry-rigged apparatus, full of gaps and easily manipulated. People have a pronounced tendency to miss things that are happening right in front of them. We do not take in our surroundings so much as actively and constantly construct them. At a major conference in Las Vegas last year, psychologists argued that magicians have been engaging in cutting-edge, if informal, research into how we see and comprehend the world around us.[4] They considered that a better understanding of magicians and their techniques could offer insight into the behavioral and neural basis of consciousness itself.[5]

There is a particular kind of experience that is provoked by aesthetic indeterminacy around material appearance. *Now You See It* is about the magical moment of transformation and what happens to viewers in the presence of such uncertainty. They may experience something and nothing, dismissal and hope, epiphany and failure.

Some people believe only in the tactile, the here and now, and that any sort of "now you don't" is pure illusion. Others believe in the ability to know the unseen. The search for something outside our immediate reality extends across time and belief. In an essay on shamanist magic, writer Michael Taussig acknowledges that "the real skill of the practitioner lies not in skilled concealment but in the skilled revelation of skilled concealment.... Hence, power flows not from masking but from an unmasking which masks more than masking does."[6] By letting the viewer in on the secret, the magic of the secret is further reinforced. This magical transformation occurs simultaneously across visuality and consciousness. What we see morphs, by an alchemical process of visuality, into something more than it was initially.

Visibility and visual recognition are intimately connected to our understanding of an object's materiality. But how do we know what an object "is," of what it is really made? Although this question is often posed as a struggle between content and form, *Now You See It* features work that forces us to reexamine our basic assumptions about how we interpret the essence of an artwork's materials. Ralph Rugoff wrote that "art...ultimately exists through our thought and reflection, and in the unseen spaces that we carry within us. [A]rt...lives on in the uses we make of it—a potentially endless process by which, conceivably, we can alter the ways we see the world and shape the world we see."[7] Addressing temporality, immediacy, and perception, *Now You See It* is an exhibition about absence and presence, being and nothingness, simultaneous duality, literalism, the thing as itself and something else altogether.

Wade Guyton's untitled inkjet-on-linen works (Fig. 1) are the contemporary equivalent of Reinhardt's *Black Paintings*. Their large, human scale creates a dark plane of space with which viewers can visually meld. The works seem to be created almost as if by mistake. The mechanically produced "paintings" are made with an Epson UltraChrome printer that allows the ink to build, leak, and get dragged and tracked across the linen. Presented with more of this overwhelming blackness, accidentally created, viewers have an opportunity to see blindness itself as a chosen mistake.

In Saramago's text, the blindness was white, rather than black. Robert Ryman's white paintings (Fig. 2), for which he is best known, can be seen as a rejoinder to the blackness of Reinhardt's and Guyton's. A substantial portion of *Now You See It* examines the use of particular mediums scaled back to their basic qualities. Ryman presents paint as paint, exploring the materials and properties of what makes a painting, a painting. The artist asks: how are paintings made, what are they made of, how are they installed in gallery and museum spaces, and how are these works experienced by those who encounter them? He exploits and explores a range of painting's inherent, contextual qualities—including surface, support, medium, placement before the viewer, and, importantly, color—to gain the answers. Ryman's paintings reveal their making. He often makes the hanging systems of his works visible and significant, extending his creative exploration beyond the edges of the picture plane. The metal fasteners and Scotch tape he uses serve both a practical and an aesthetic purpose, linking the paintings to the rest of the world and challenging traditional notions of the frame and pictorial space. By extending the paintings into the realm of the viewer, he impacts and affects that space. If the pictorial arena expands infinitely, does art consequently, and hopefully positively, impact the social space of life?

Light can also be blinding. The entire photographic process depends on light, and Walead Beshty captures its essence (Fig. 3). His photographs depict their own making, revealing the magic of their creation. Beshty folds up photographic paper and exposes it to light. The paper is then unfolded and processed, creating abstract planes of color (or darkness) intersecting with blankness. The white spaces directly illustrate the void into which the light failed to travel.

Gedi Sibony has been termed "an alchemist of the everyday."[8] He takes seemingly valueless domestic construction materials and transforms them into something else, something sometimes aesthetic, sometimes surprising, sometimes magical (Fig. 3). Sibony works with carpet, garbage bags, foam insulation, MDF, hollow-core doors, sticks, and levels or blinds. Many are castoffs, chosen for their familiarity and ubiquity, and patched together into haphazard forms. Despite the beauty and seduction of the resulting objects, the impossibility of actual transformation is inherent in the work. We hope what we see is more than what it actually is. We believe that objects assembled by someone with a specific intention can cause a transformation, an imbuing of aura into something culled from the mundane. We hope all of this while acknowledging that it probably will not, probably can not. But, still, there is an open-ended question, a maybe. How great would it be to conjure that possibility? As such, Sibony's work tests the limits of our faith in art, while simultaneously renewing it.

As part of an ongoing interaction between artists Robert Morris and John Cage, the latter attempted to impress upon Morris the observation that "most of what happens never was in anybody's mind."[9] While Cage was comfortable with a reductive simplicity regarding the interaction between viewer and object, Morris needed to maintain a consciousness-based element to his work. But the question of just where the consciousness is located is perhaps more compelling. Can it be located within the object, or just within the viewer? Is its presence important, or is it the idea of its presence that is important? Is the existence identified through its absence?

Morris's felt work *Vetti V* (1993) cascades down the wall and pools on the floor, challenging the thick, structured fabric to flow elegantly with the quality of a wholly different substance. Peeled away at the center, the work reveals first gray, then pink, and suggests the interior of a feminine form, despite Morris's commitment to Minimalism's non-referential stance.

Many of the artists included in the exhibition are concerned with the role that art objects play in the world. Lawrence Weiner has stated that art is about material objects: "Art, when it's placed into the context of the world, is not just used in the context of what we know as art history; it is an attempt to place material which could be used to enrich the daily lives of other human beings."[10] Weiner's *A 36" X 36" REMOVAL TO THE LATHING OR SUPPORT WALL OF PLASTER OR WALL BOARD FROM A WALL* (1968; Fig. 4) directly acknowledges the basis of visuality and art. The work is simply the removal of a square piece of a gallery wall, intended to reveal what is underneath. It is dumb geometry. The work is both humorous and insightful, addressing how and what we see, as well as what lies waiting to be seen just beneath the surface.

Fred Sandback has explained that when he began to use string, he "want[ed] to be able to make sculpture that didn't have an inside."[11] He explored phenomenological geometry, adding, "I don't see various sculptures so much as being discrete objects.... The idea was to have the work right there along with everything else in the world.... It had utopian glimmerings of art and life happily cohabiting."[12] Because Sandback's sculptures are so visually subtle, the moment they appear to the viewer creates a fissure. The art exists in the space of the viewer, unnoticed, until a precise moment. The accompanying recognition produces the moment of consciousness.

Ceal Floyer's witty conceptualism is manifested in exceedingly simple optical plays. In *Door* (1995; Fig. 5), Floyer points a slide projector at the base of an interior door, throwing a horizontal band of light along the bottom edge. The subtlety of the effect is that it appears as if the light is emanating from the other side rather than from superficial projection. In the video *Ink on Paper* (1999), the artist puts a marker to paper and lets all of the ink bleed out. The circle of ink radiates outward. The duration of the work is the amount of ink in the pen.

In a 1997 interview, Tom Friedman remarked, "I was thinking about how one's knowledge of the history behind something affects one's thinking about that thing."[13] That year, he completed *1,000 Hours of Staring* (1992–97), in which he spent more than one thousand hours staring at a thirty-two-inch-square piece of white paper. Not only exploring how the meaning of an ordinary object is transformed by contextual information, Friedman also creates a work of magical minimalism in which viewers must ascertain the veracity of the object solely through their own system of belief. Perception—including the limits of our senses and how our brain is hardwired to make sense of our daily environment—is central to Friedman's practice. Only once an object is placed in a gallery does it obtain significance. When that object is something not usually elevated, the viewer can come away puzzled. *Two by Four* (1990) is a two-by-four leaning against the wall and painted to look exactly like itself. Its placement in the gallery, coupled with the trompe l'oeil finish, causes viewers to pause. Floyer and Friedman both pursue phenomenological dumbness.

Jennifer West exposes film to a variety of physical and chemical circumstances and encounters. The titles of her works hint at these processes, and they reveal the application of unusual materials to the emulsion. *Green M&M's & Mezcal Worm Film (70MM film leader with a mescal worm dragged over the surface—imprinted with hundreds of green M&M's)* (2008; Fig. 6) projects an abstract field of green worms and dots. West's works record the performative nature of her process. The actions she takes are implicit in creating the works and imbuing them with a physical, as well as organic, residue. West has stated, "Film is inherently alchemical, as it's made of layers of emulsion that are exposed to light or in my case, anything I want, that then produces 'gold' in the form of mesmerizing, colorful images."[14]

Erwin Wurm uses materials that embody characteristics of prior use, thereby becoming visual tools by which resemblance can be organized and identified. The artist explains the origin of his use of everyday materials as a response to financial constraints when he was a student. He was forced to work with inexpensive materials, things discarded by other people, including clothing and even dust. Wurm uses dust to record absence. It is a way of referencing both time and memory. As Walter Benjamin has observed, we see the new within the always-the-same and the always-the-same within the new. Wurm accomplishes this by suggesting a new reality when material is re-formed.

Rudolf Stingel's untitled work from 2002, a shimmering, silver monochrome, is actually a large piece of Celotex insulation board. The imperfections scratched into the surface are the result of viewer interaction. Using coins, keys, pencils, or anything else that can be found, people leave the residue of their presence in the form of graffiti-like markings. Stingel

Fig. 1

Fig. 2

Fig. 3

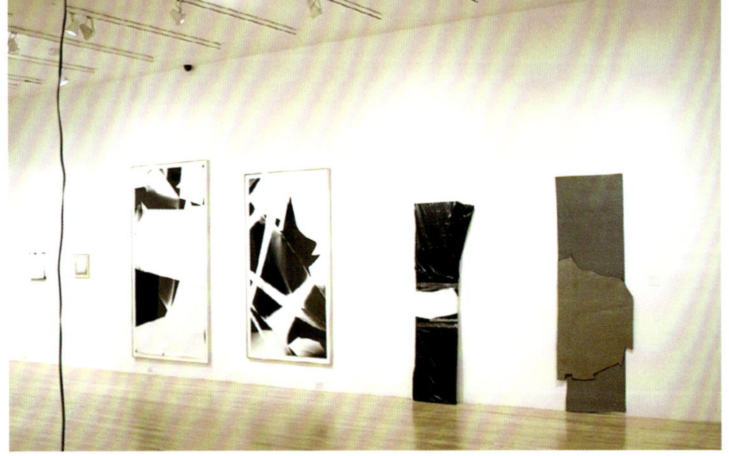

Fig. 4

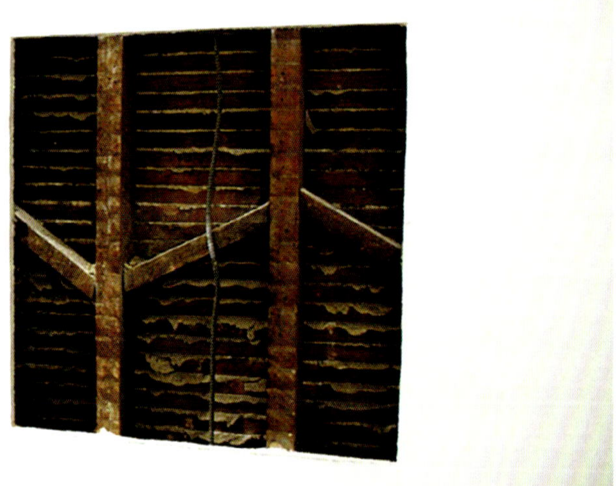

Fig. 5

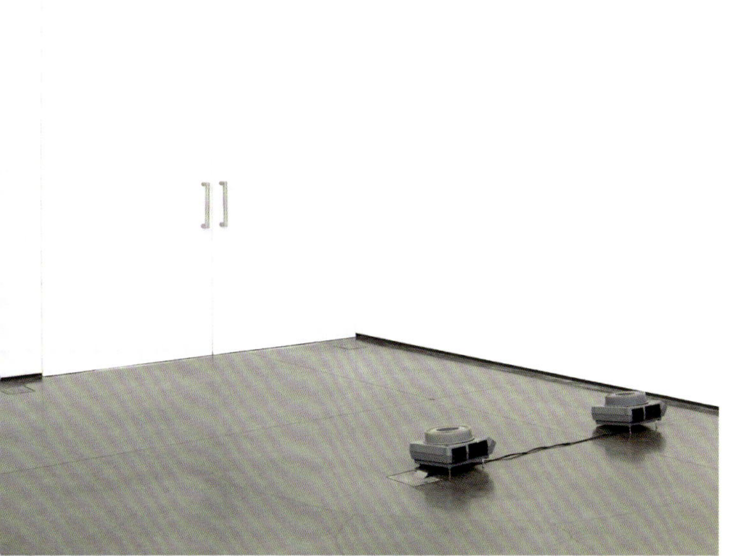

Fig. 6

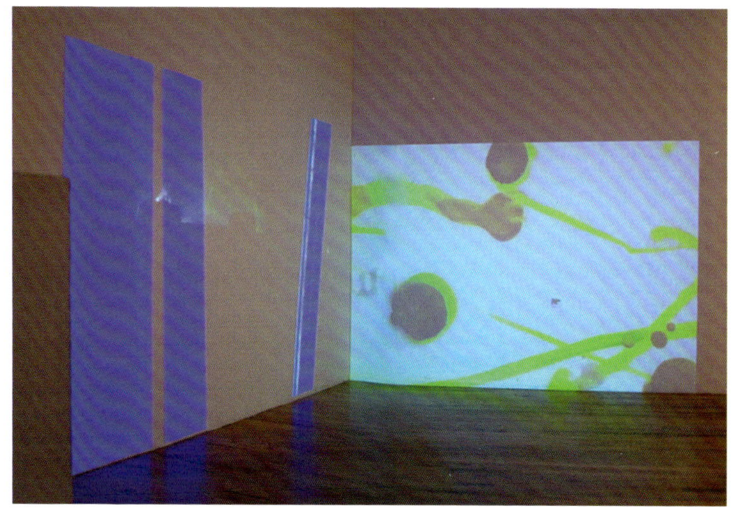

Fig. 7

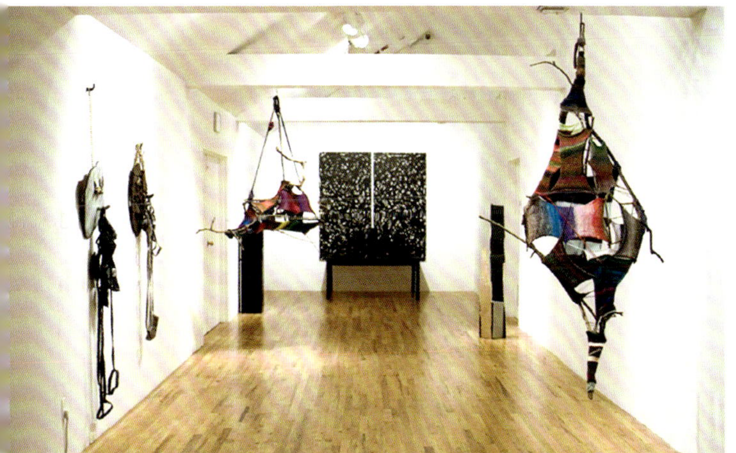

Fig. 8

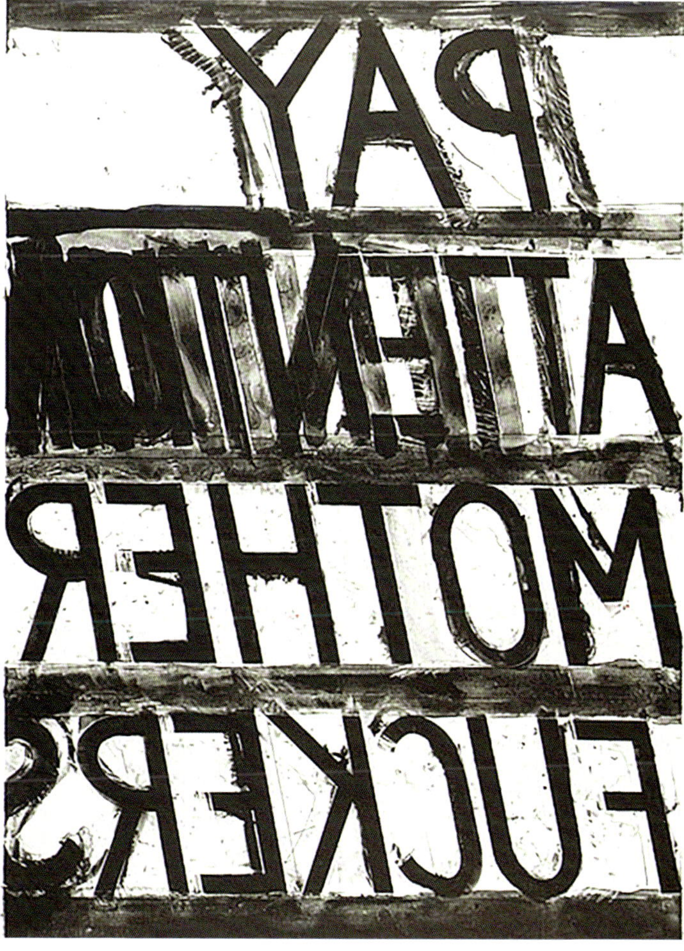

complicates the modernist form of large-scale monochromatic painting, trading paint on canvas for material that is significantly mundane and potentially even toxic. Stingel's material reveals its own history while simultaneously conveying the active role that we, as viewers, can play in transformation, physical as well as conscious.

The idea of transformation is also at the heart of Wolfgang Laib's practice. Laib utilizes natural materials such as pollen, milk, and beeswax, removed from their natural environment, in order to illuminate their essence. He has explained, "I think the better the art is…the more it really makes a change to something else."[15] In thinking about human progress, Laib eloquently stated, "From day to day or year to year it may have been the politicians who marched into another country or did this and that, but eventually it was culture which somehow brought mankind to somewhere else."[16]

Laib's *Milkstones* appear to be solid pieces of pure white marble. With careful viewing, however, the non-static surface becomes noticeable, where a finely balanced concavity has been created from milk being poured to the exact point of suspension. When we realize that something is not as we thought, the opportunity for transcendence opens up. This possibility—and its always-present counter, impossibility—sanctions the notion that art can, as Laib suggests, positively change the world.

Felix Gonzalez-Torres worked with objects just as they are, for example, lightbulbs and plastic beads. The installation, and even the sourcing of the materials, are left to the exhibitor. The light strands evoke various references—from safety to spirituality to impermanence—depending on how they are installed, either suspended from the ceiling or lying on the floor, indoors or outside, stretched in a clean line or messily gathered. Gonzalez-Torres's works are inspired by everyday events, personal biography, and the challenges of late-twentieth-century life. In an interview with Robert Nickas, the artist stated, "Meaning is created once something can be related to personal experience."[17] Gonzalez-Torres created works that necessitate viewer participation. By generously offering the viewer a role in the work, both in its perception and in the construction of its meaning, the experience becomes deeply personal.

Dieter Roth is also known for utilizing pedestrian materials, although often he employs elements prone to decomposition, questioning their nature and sustainability: cheese, chocolate, rabbit droppings, tar, glue, cocoa powder, sour milk, moldy foods, and licorice sticks, among them. By employing found objects, Roth facilitates the viewer's remembrance of their past use and function. The resulting insight into the choices of materials allows viewers to align their perceptions with that of the artist. Because they recognize what they are looking at materially, the perceptual acknowledgment of visual alchemy is resounding for viewers. Roth's is a mythic materiality.

Alexandra Bircken assembles natural elements, such as sticks and twigs, and wraps them with brightly colored yarn (Fig. 7). Often suspended from the ceiling or attached to the wall, these orblike objects resemble tumors, growths, or other biomorphic disfigurations, camouflaged by aestheticized decoration.

Similarly, Anna Sew Hoy combines diverse materials in an idiosyncratic way. She focuses on odd circular ceramic elements through and upon which other elements are added, threaded, or suspended. She utilizes chains and denim to create pieces that are simultaneously anthropomorphic—visually as well as with titles such as *Heart* and *Two Eyes* (both 2007; Fig. 7)—and abstract. Each work hangs on the wall supported by a single screw, evoking a Native American dream catcher, car and house keys, or a character from an L. Frank Baum novel. As Hoy herself has commented, "I zoom in on the object and try to give it a new life, realize its potential to be transformed and to achieve new meaning or significance."[18]

Mitzi Pederson employs simple, raw materials and combines them in unexpected, enchanting ways. Her untitled piece from 2008 bears an intriguing relationship to Friedman's *Two by Four*, as here, Pederson also uses a piece of wood that is leaned against a wall. Pederson's wood is just that, though, with the subtle addition of silver leaf. Another untitled work, made of a cinder block, wood, sand, glue, and string, is intentionally modest in its materials, while mimicking classical modernist sculptural forms. Its charm lies in the small length of blue string that stretches across the vertical lengths. Its extension and connection are more like an elegant spider's web than a piece of structural support. Pederson transforms these utilitarian materials through the additive nature of collage. The items she uses are independent objects, but together, become something more.

The work that William O'Brien created specifically for *Now You See It* suggests a complex, insular world engulfed by a dark cover (Fig. 7). A grouping of mildly figurative objects cowers together on a low, black table set against a cosmically oriented drawing. While the image could suggest a poetic nightscape, it also recalls the blindness, here black rather than white, of Saramago. Again, the notion of rewarding a lingering view is implied. Our engagement deepens beyond the initial seduction. Sometimes, when staring at a work of art, we leave the place in which we have been and end up somewhere previously unimaginable.

Seeing is often believing. We want to be shown evidence to verify truth. Once inside the asylum, Saramago's characters, now blind, must trust in things that they also cannot see. The blindness necessitates turning to other means to navigate their existences. Seeing is intimately connected to our notions of truth, and in fact, it underpins our belief in the world around us. The bias toward the visual reached an apotheosis of sorts in the mid-1960s when Frank Stella formulated his famous "What you see is what you see" credo. One of the pioneers of Minimalism, Stella declared that, in his paintings, there was nothing "besides the paint on the canvas" and insisted that "only what can be seen there is there."[19] His perspective seems to come right out of Ryman's own insistence.

Describing the rationale of her work, Louise Bourgeois explained, "It is all there because of the energy. Passing from one state to another, or the transformations."[20] She also recognizes, at the core of her work, "The resistance of the material corresponds to the insistence on coming to the core of the matter, it is an exact replica of the compulsion to understand."[21] Those efforts to see, know, be seen, and be known are a driving force for effort, interaction, and creation in art and in life.

Bruce Nauman, in one of his first neon works from 1967—a medium identified with commercial visual culture—proclaims, "The true artist helps the world by revealing mystic truths." Five years later, he created a limited-edition print that can be understood as a mantra for art that demands our awareness: "Pay Attention Mother Fuckers" (Fig. 8). But, if we, as viewers, do not pay attention, what do we miss? Not only might we miss the subtle blues in a Reinhardt, the seemingly impossible balance in a Sibony, or the aura of a Friedman, we might also, in fact, be blind to something greater: the ability to perceive beyond the here and now. Magic—whether in the sleight of hand of skilled magicians or the phenomenological play of visual artists—allows us to see it now. Once something is revealed (again) after it disappeared or was rendered invisible, the inherent value ascends. After we stand in the space of unknowing, witnessing the aesthetic indeterminacy and seeking the embodied magic, what we may walk away knowing is that blindness is now an impossibility.

NOTES

1 José Saramago, *Blindness* (Lisbon: Caminho, 1997), 292.

2 Ad Reinhardt quoted in Lucy Lippard, "Introduction to 557,087" in *Conceptual Art: A Critical Anthology*, ed. Alexander Alberro and Blake Stimson (Cambridge, MA: MIT Press, 1999), 184.

3 *New York Times* art critic Holland Cotter wrote, "The primary reward [these paintings] offered was the experience of being with them, which, to be an experience...required patience and concentration," in Holland Cotter, "Tall, Dark and Fragile," <http://www.nytimes.com/2008/08/01/arts/design/01blac.html> (accessed August 1, 2008).

4 Drake Bennett, "How magicians control your mind: Magic isn't just a bag of tricks—it's a finely tuned technology for shaping what we see. How researchers are extracting its lessons," <http://www.boston.com> (accessed August 3, 2008).

5 Stephen L. Macknik, Mac King, James Randi, Apollo Robbins, Teller, John Thompson, and Susana Martinez-Conde, "Attention and awareness in stage magic: Turning tricks into research," in *Nature Review Neuroscience*, July 30, 2008, 1.

6 Anthony Huberman, "I (not love) Information," in *Afterall* 16 (Autumn/Winter 2007), 23.

7 Ralph Rugoff, *A Brief History of Invisible Art* (San Francisco: CCA Wattis Institute for Contemporary Arts, 2005), 17.

8 "Gedi Sibony," in *New Yorker*, May 26, 2008.

9 Claes Oldenburg, Andy Warhol, Robert Morris, and Benjamin H. D. Buchloh, "Three Conversations in 1985: Claes Oldenburg, Andy Warhol, Robert Morris," in *Duchamp Effect*, October 70 (Autumn 1994), 64.

10 Lynne Cooke, "Lawrence Weiner Displacement," Dia Art Foundation, <http://www.diaart.org> (accessed August 3, 2008).

11 Fred Sandback, "Remarks on My Sculpture," Dia Art Foundation, <http://www.diachelsea.org> (accessed August 3, 2008).
12 Ibid.
13 Ron Platt, *Tom Friedman* (Winston-Salem: Southeastern Center for Contemporary Art), 5.
14 Greg Kurcewicz, "Jennifer West Interview," <http://www.kurcewicz.co.uk> (accessed May 23, 2008).
15 Darren James Jorgensen, "Wolfgang Laib: Returning to What Is, an Interview with Wolfgang Laib," *e-maj* (July–December 2005), 5.4.
16 Ibid.
17 Robert Nickas, "Felix Gonzalez-Torres: All the Time in the World," *Flash Art* 246 <https://www.flashartonline.com/article/felix-gonzalez-torres/> (accessed August 3, 2008).
18 Artist Statement, Asia Society, *One Way or Another: Asian American Art Show*, <http://sites.asiasociety.org/arts/onewayoranother/oneway3.html> (accessed August 3, 2008).
19 Ralph Rugoff, A *Brief History of Invisible Art* (San Francisco: CCA Wattis Institute for Contemporary Arts, 2005), 8.
20 Francis Morris, ed., *Louise Bourgeois* (Tate Modern, London, and the Museum of Contemporary Art, Los Angeles), 174.
21 Ibid.

LIST OF ILLUSTRATIONS

Fig. 1
Wade Guyton, Untitled, 2007. Epson UltraChrome inkjet on linen, 84 x 69 in (213.4 x 175.3 cm). Collection of Warren and Allison Kanders. Courtesy the artist and Petzel, New York

Fig. 2
Robert Ryman, *Series #22 (White)*, 2004. Oil on canvas, 16 x 16 in (40.6 x 40.6 cm). Collection of Susan and Larry Marx. © Robert Ryman. Courtesy PaceWildenstein, New York. © 2018 Robert Ryman / Artist Rights Society (ARS), New York

Fig. 3 L–R:
Walead Beshty, *Fold (Three Directional Light Sources, 35/62.5/145 degrees), December 22nd, 2006, Valencia, CA, Ilford Multigrade Fiber IV*, 2007; Walead Beshty, *Fold (80 degree directional light source) November 27th, 2006, Valencia, CA, Ilford, Multigrade fiber IV*, 2007; Gedi Sibony, *The Last One*, 2008; Gedi Sibony, *Left So Soon*, 2008. Installation view: *Now You See It*, Aspen Art Museum, 2008

Fig. 4
Lawrence Weiner, *A 36" X 36" REMOVAL TO THE LATHING OR SUPPORT WALL OF PLASTER OR WALLBOARD FROM A WALL*, 1968. Installation view: *Pocket Utopia*, Brooklyn, 2007. Courtesy the Siegelaub Collection & Archives at the Stichting Egress Foundation, Amsterdam. Photo: James Wagner (jameswagner.com). © 2018 Lawrence Weiner / Artist Rights Society (ARS), New York

Fig. 5
Ceal Floyer, *Door*, 1999. Installation view: Aspen Art Museum, 2016. Photo: Tony Prikryl

Fig. 6
Jennifer West, *Green M&M's & Mezcal Worm Film (70 mm film leader with a mescal worm dragged over the surface—imprinted with hundreds of green M&M's)*, 2008. Installation view: *Now You See It*, Aspen Art Museum, 2008

Fig. 7 L–R:
Anna Sew Hoy, *Two Eyes*, 2007; Anna Sew Hoy, *Heart*, 2007; Alexandra Bircken, *Ship*, 2007; William O'Brien, Untitled, 2008; Alexandra Bircken, *Spindel*, 2007. Installation view: *Now You See It*, Aspen Art Museum, 2008

Fig. 8
Bruce Nauman, *Pay Attention*, 1973. Lithograph on Arjomari paper, 38 1/4 x 28 1/4 in (97.2 x 71.8 cm). © 2018 Bruce Nauman and Gemini G.E.L. / Artist Rights Society (ARS), New York

Douglas Fogle
On the Road with Catherine Opie

Catherine Opie's entire artistic career can be seen as one long road trip across this continent in search not of the American dream, but rather a dream of an idea of American community. When I first met the photographer in 1998, she was driving across the country in a late-model camper van with her dog, Nika. She had stopped in Minneapolis to shoot part of her series *Domestic*, which documents lesbian couples, families, and friends in their households. Her three-month odyssey from Los Angeles to New York, with stops in Oklahoma, North Carolina, and Minnesota, resulted in powerful and dignified portrayals of her subjects in the realm of a profoundly recognizable domesticity. What struck me in the wake of Opie's visit, as she unplugged her camper from the outlet in my apartment and set off on the remainder of her trip, was that how one captures the American cultural landscape fascinates the artist as much as the character of those communities.

Opie began her journey in Los Angeles in 1993 with her formal, color-saturated portraits of friends in the lesbian and gay leather community. She then meandered throughout the architectural circulatory system of Southern California in her 1994 *Freeway* series, whose haunting images of empty highway overpasses constitute a veritable paean to an arterial system of travel in which community is defined by the temporality of movement. In 1995, leaving the Santa Monica, San Diego, and Pasadena freeways behind, Opie exited into the neighborhoods of Hollywood on her way to the tonier parts of Los Angeles. It was here that she made a number of house calls, photographing idiosyncratic features on the façades of Beverly Hills and Bel Air homes. The resulting figureless portraits are every bit as revelatory of specific characters as her work with posed human subjects.

In 1997, not yet ready to leave the West Coast, Opie took a drive down Sunset Boulevard in order to document that ubiquitous piece of distinctly American vernacular architecture, the mini-mall. Like her photographs of freeways and Beverly Hills homes, her black-and-white panoramic images of these banal neighborhood structures were devoid of obvious human presence while being completely suggestive of it. As the artist herself states: "[They] mark the entrance and exits of various populations. They are not like mini-malls in the suburbs, which have chains like Starbucks and Jamba Juice. These are about the American dream for me. But they're very fragile. They change almost overnight, and are often forgotten about, just like the freeways."[1]

The connective tissue that bridges the gap between Opie's seemingly divergent bodies of work is a question about America. How does one even begin to think about taking a portrait of a nation? This problem has been posed by photographers for more than a century, and Swiss-born émigré Robert Frank attempted to answer it with his book *The Americans*, first published in France in 1958. His photographic tour of the United States took place in 1955 and resulted in stark and biting images of American community: picnics, Fourth of July celebrations, automobiles, roadside restaurants, Hollywood premieres, and of course, the highway. As Walker Evans wrote, “Frank shows a high irony toward a nation that, generally speaking, has it not.”[2] He himself had earlier taken another route in his collaboration with writer James Agee when they produced their 1941 book *Let Us Now Praise Famous Men*, which poetically and forcefully documented the impoverished lives of three Alabama families during the Depression. Evans depicted the plight of tenant farmers in the 1930s by producing powerful images of a community at risk.

Frank and Evans engaged in physical and metaphorical road trips across the nation in their quest to capture the quintessence of the American experience. Frank’s subject matter was broader and his approach was laced with an ironic detachment, while Evans’s focus was more specific and characterized by a sense of dignified humanism. For Opie, however, it is not so much a question of discovering some elusive universal essence that is uniquely American, since no one body of images can distill something as quixotic as that identity. In her work, it is more a question of constructing a mosaic from a series of individual parts that somehow coalesce to create a fragmented whole. Her search for another piece of this picture brought the artist back to Minneapolis.

In 2000, Opie put together an artist book focusing on American cities that she called *East, Middle, West*. While this was a single work devoted specifically to images of the Williamsburg Bridge in New York, the St. Louis Gateway Arch, and the mountainous California landscape, we might take its title as a metaphor for the artist’s photographic career. If *Freeways* and *Mini-malls* could stand in for her interpretation of the character of Los Angeles and hence be her “West,” what would be her “Middle”? Her “East”? After completing a group of black-and-white panoramic photographs documenting the former site of the 1904 World’s Fair in St. Louis, she returned to the Twin Cities in 2000 to begin a yearlong artist-in-residence project at the Walker Art Center. Conceptually moving up the Mississippi from St. Louis, she would try to further identify her “Middle” in the Upper Midwest. Once in Minneapolis, her interest turned again to finding the photographic zero degree of the community. Having already attempted to capture something of its character with portraiture in her *Domestic* series, Opie returned to architecture....

Filmmakers like John Ford etched their vision of the American landscape into our collective psyches in movies like *The Searchers* (1956) by repeatedly offering us long shots of iconic vistas such as Monument Valley, Utah. Through her photographic projects, Opie traces a path along the conceptual horizon line that is America, but she does so with a diversity of means across a much wider body of subjects. In the end, these images speak both a formal language of vision and social language of community and attempt to answer the question of how one represents a nation....

I began this...with a personal anecdote about the artist because I believe there is something incredibly humanistic about her work. Whether producing photographic portraits of human subjects or unpopulated architectural studies, she demonstrates a regard for the social that extends beyond the confines of her carefully measured photographic formalism.

NOTES

1 Russell Ferguson, "'How I Think': An Interview with Catherine Opie," in Kate Bush, ed., *Catherine Opie* (London: The Photographer's Gallery, 2000), 48.

2 Quoted in Beaumont Newhall, *The History of Photography* (New York: Museum of Modern Art, 1982), 288. Originally published in Tom Maloney, ed., *US Camera* (New York: US Camera Publishing Company, 1958), 90.

Untitled #1 (Surfers), 2003. C-print, 50 x 40 in (127 x 101.6 cm).

Untitled #2 (Surfers), 2003. C-print, 50 x 40 in (127 x 101.6

[CO.2010]

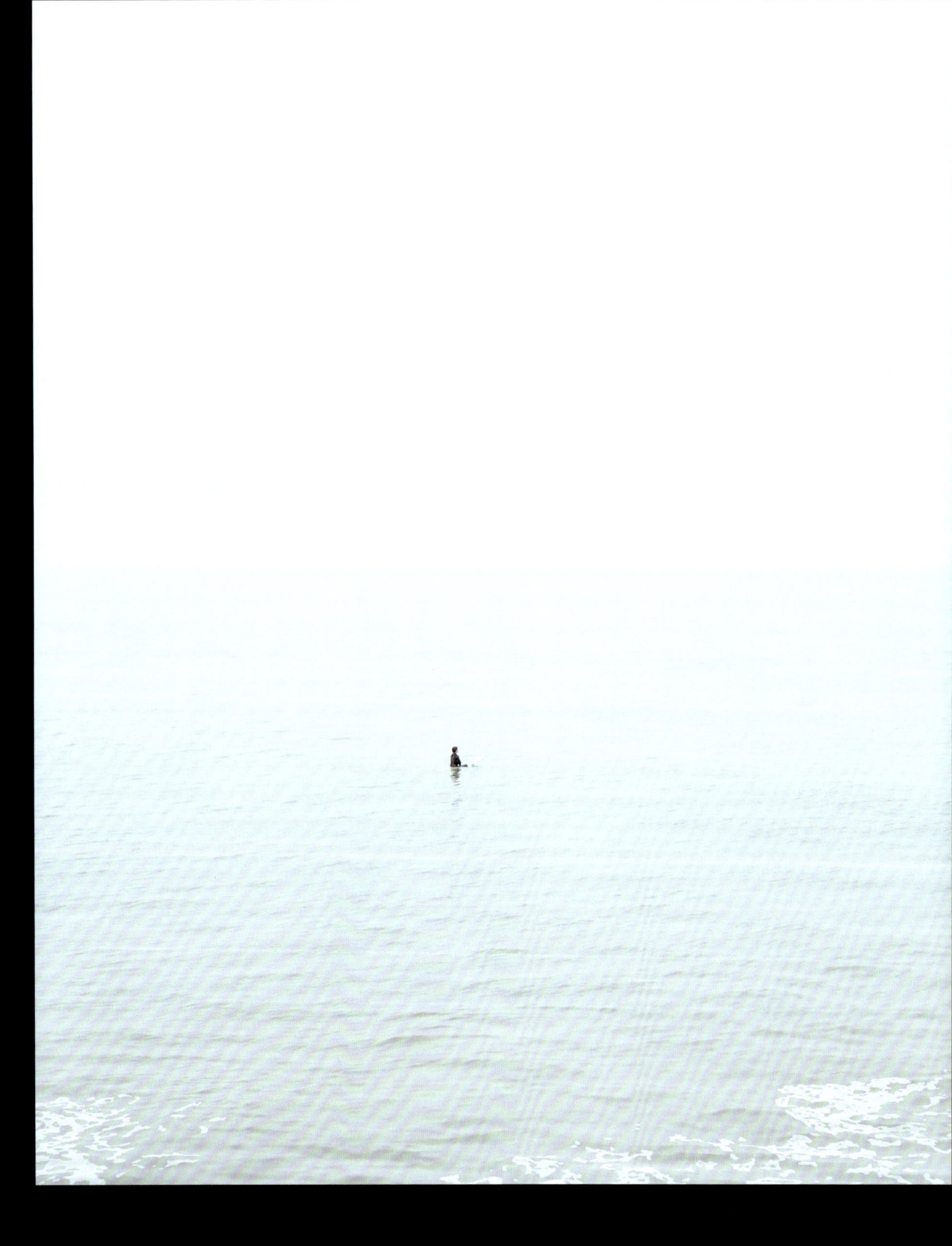

Untitled #6 (Surfers), 2003. C-print, 50 x 40 in (127 x 10

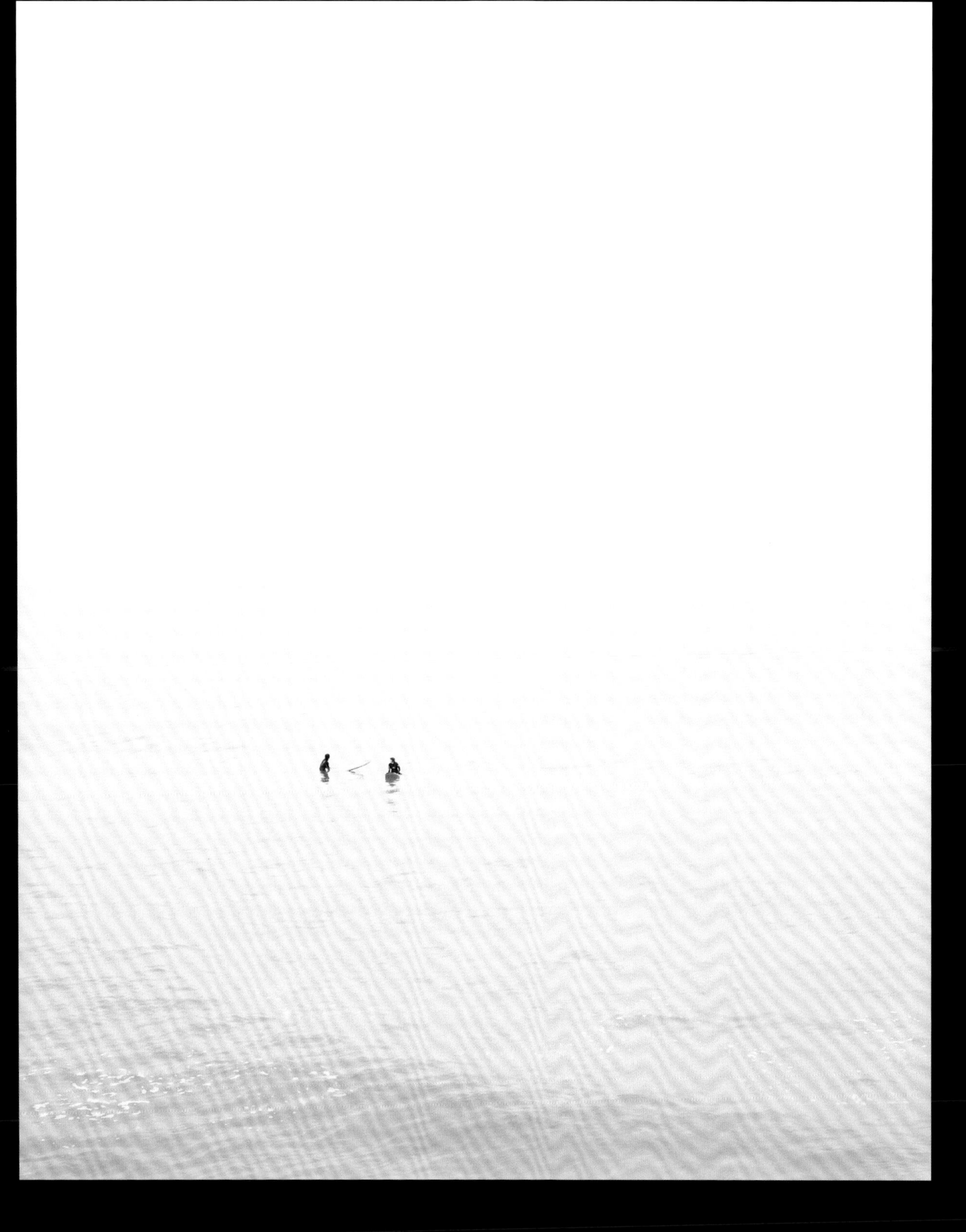

Untitled #8 (Surfers), 2003. C-print, 50 x 40 in (127 x 101.6 cm)

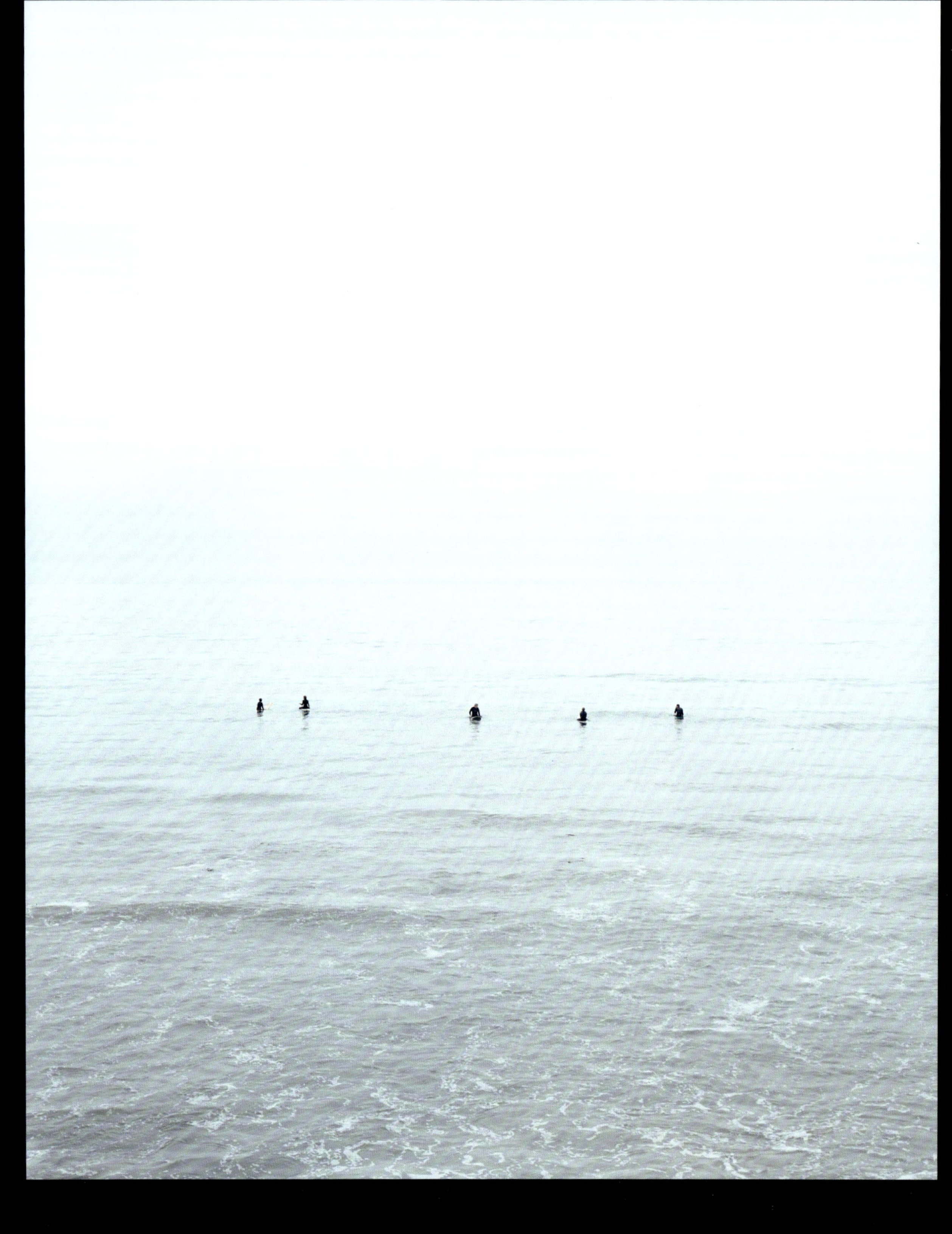

Untitled #10 (Surfers), 2003. C-print, 50 x 40 in (127 x 101.

[CO.2010]

Untitled #14 (Surfers), 2003. C-print, 50 x 40 in (127 x 101.6 cm)

David Foster Wallace
This is Water

There are these two young fish swimming along, and they happen to meet an older fish swimming the other way, who nods at them and says, "Morning, boys, how's the water?" And the two young fish swim on for a bit, and then eventually, one of them looks over at the other and goes, "What the hell is water?"

If at this moment, you're worried that I plan to present myself here as the wise old fish explaining what water is to you younger fish, please don't be. I am not the wise old fish. The immediate point of the fish story is that the most obvious, ubiquitous, important realities are often the ones that are the hardest to see and talk about. Stated as an English sentence, of course, this is just a banal platitude—but the fact is that, in the day-to-day trenches of adult existence, banal platitudes can have life-or-death importance. That may sound like hyperbole, or abstract nonsense.

A huge percentage of the stuff that I tend to be automatically certain of is, it turns out, totally wrong and deluded. Here's one example of the utter wrongness of something I tend to be automatically sure of: everything in my own immediate experience supports my deep belief that I am the absolute center of the universe, the realest, most vivid and important person in existence. We rarely talk about this sort of natural, basic self-centeredness, because it's so socially repulsive, but it's pretty much the same for all of us, deep down. It is our default-setting, hard-wired into our boards at birth. Think about it: there is no experience you've had that you were not at the absolute center of. The world as you experience it is right there in front of you, or behind you, to the left or right of you, on your TV, or your monitor, or whatever. Other people's thoughts and feelings have to be communicated to you somehow, but your own are so immediate, urgent, *real*—you get the idea. But please don't worry that I'm getting ready to preach to you about compassion or other-directedness or the so-called "virtues." This is not a matter of virtue—it's a matter of my choosing to do the work of somehow altering or getting free of my natural, hard-wired default-setting, which is to be deeply and literally self-centered, and to see and interpret everything through this lens of self.

People who can adjust their natural default-setting this way are often described as being "well adjusted," which I suggest to you is not an accidental term.

Given the triumphal academic setting here, an obvious question is how much of this work of adjusting our default-setting involves actual knowledge or intellect. This question gets tricky. Probably the most dangerous thing about college education, at least in my own case, is that it enables my tendency to over-intellectualize stuff, to get lost in abstract arguments inside my head instead of simply paying attention to what's going on right in front of me. Paying attention to what's going on inside me. As I'm sure you guys know by now, it is extremely difficult to stay alert and attentive instead of getting hypnotized by the constant monologue inside your own head. Twenty years after my own graduation, I have come gradually to understand that the liberal-arts cliché about "teaching you how to think" is actually shorthand for a much deeper, more serious idea: "Learning how to think" really means learning how to exercise some control over how and what you think. It means being conscious and aware enough to choose what you pay attention to and to choose how you construct meaning from experience. Because if you cannot exercise this kind of choice in adult life, you will be totally hosed. Think of the old cliché about "the mind being an excellent servant but a terrible master." This, like many clichés, so lame and unexciting on the surface, actually expresses a great and terrible truth. It is not the least bit coincidental that adults who commit suicide with firearms almost always shoot themselves in the head. And the truth is that most of these suicides are actually dead long before they pull the trigger. And I submit that this is what the real, no-bull-value of your liberal-arts education is supposed to be about: how to keep from going through your comfortable, prosperous, respectable adult life dead, unconscious, a slave to your head and to your natural default-setting of being uniquely, completely, imperially alone, day in and day out.

That may sound like hyperbole, or abstract nonsense. So let's get concrete. The plain fact is that you graduating seniors do not yet have any clue what "day in, day out" really means. There happen to be whole large parts of adult American life that nobody talks about in commencement speeches. One such part involves boredom, routine, and petty frustration. The parents and older folks here will know all too well what I'm talking about.

By way of example, let's say it's an average day, and you get up in the morning, go to your challenging job, and you work hard for nine or ten hours, and at the end of the day, you're tired, and you're stressed out, and all you want is to go home and have a good supper and maybe unwind for a couple of hours and then hit the rack early because you have to get up the next day and do it all again. But then you remember there's no food at home—you haven't had time to shop this week, because of your challenging job—and so now, after work, you have to get in your car and drive to the supermarket. It's the end of the workday, and the traffic's very bad, so getting to the store takes way longer than it should, and when you finally get there, the supermarket is very crowded, because, of course, it's the time of day when all the other people with jobs also try to squeeze in some grocery shopping, and the store's hideously, fluorescently lit, and infused with soul-killing Muzak or corporate pop, and it's pretty much the last place you want to be, but you can't just get in and quickly out: you have to wander all over the huge, overlit store's crowded aisles to find the stuff you want, and you have to maneuver your junky cart through all these other tired, hurried people with carts, and, of course, there are also the glacially slow old people and the spacey people and the ADHD kids who all block the aisle and you have to grit your teeth and try to be polite as you ask them to let you by, and eventually, finally, you get all your supper supplies, except now it turns out there aren't enough checkout lanes open even though it's the end-of-the-day rush, so the checkout line is incredibly long, which is stupid and infuriating, but you can't take your fury out on the frantic lady working the register.

Anyway, you finally get to the checkout line's front, and pay for your food, and wait to get your check or card authenticated by a machine, and then get told to "Have a nice day" in a voice that is the absolute voice of death, and then you have to take your creepy flimsy plastic bags of groceries in your cart through the crowded, bumpy, littery parking lot, and try to load the bags in your car in such a way that everything doesn't fall out of the bags and roll around in the trunk on the way home, and then you have to drive all the way home through slow, heavy, SUV-intensive rush-hour traffic, et cetera, et cetera.

The point is that petty, frustrating crap like this is exactly where the work of choosing comes in. Because the traffic jams and crowded aisles and long checkout lines give me time to think, and if I don't make a conscious decision about how to think and what to pay attention to, I'm going to be pissed and miserable every time I have to food-shop, because my natural default-setting is the certainty that situations like this are really all about *me*, about my hungriness and my fatigue and my desire to just get home, and it's going to seem, for all the world, like everybody else is just *in my way*, and who are all these people in my way? And look at how repulsive most of them are and how stupid and cow-like and dead-eyed and nonhuman they seem here in the checkout line, or at how annoying and rude it is that people are talking loudly on cell phones in the middle of the line, and look at how deeply unfair this is: I've worked really hard all day and I'm starved and tired and I can't even get home to eat and unwind because of all these stupid goddamn *people*.

Or, of course, if I'm in a more socially conscious form of my default-setting, I can spend time in the end-of-the-day traffic jam being angry and disgusted at all the huge, stupid, lane-blocking SUVs and Hummers and V-12 pickup trucks burning their wasteful, selfish, forty-gallon tanks of gas, and I can dwell on the fact that the patriotic or religious bumper stickers always seem to be on the biggest, most disgustingly selfish vehicles driven by the ugliest, most inconsiderate and aggressive drivers, who are usually talking on cell phones as they cut people off in order to get just twenty stupid feet ahead in a traffic jam, and I can think about how our children's children will despise us for wasting all the future's fuel and probably screwing up the climate, and how spoiled and stupid and disgusting we all are, and how it all just *sucks*, and so on and so forth...

Look, if I choose to think this way, fine, lots of us do—except that thinking this way tends to be so easy and automatic, it doesn't *have* to be a choice. Thinking this way is my natural default-setting. It's the automatic, unconscious way that I experience the boring, frustrating, crowded parts of adult life when I'm operating on the automatic, unconscious belief that I am the center of the world and that my immediate needs and feelings are what should determine the world's priorities. The thing is that there are obviously different ways to think about these kinds of situations. In this traffic, all these vehicles stuck and idling in my way: it's not impossible that some of these people in SUVs have been in horrible auto accidents in the past and now find driving so traumatic that their therapist has all but ordered them to get a huge, heavy SUV so they can feel safe enough to drive; or that the Hummer that just cut me off is maybe being driven by a father whose little child is hurt or sick in the seat next to him, and he's trying to rush to the hospital, and he's in a way bigger, more legitimate hurry than I am—it is actually *I* who am in *his* way. Or I can choose to force myself to consider the likelihood that everyone else in the supermarket's checkout line is just as bored and frustrated as I am, and that some of these people probably have much harder, more tedious or painful lives than I do, overall.

Again, please don't think that I'm giving you moral advice, or that I'm saying you're "supposed to" think this way, or that anyone expects you to just automatically do it, because it's hard, it takes will and mental effort, and if you're like me, some days you won't be able to do it, or you just flat-out won't want to. But most days, if you're aware enough to give yourself a choice, you can choose to look differently at this fat, dead-eyed, over-made lady who just screamed at her little child in the checkout line—maybe she's not usually like this; maybe she's been up three straight nights holding the hand of her husband who's dying of bone cancer; or maybe this very lady is the low-wage clerk at the Motor Vehicles Department who just yesterday helped your spouse resolve a nightmarish red-tape problem through some small act of bureaucratic kindness. Of course, none of this is likely, but it's also not impossible—it just depends on what you want to consider. If you're automatically sure that you know what reality is and who and what is really important—if you want to operate on your default-setting—then you, like me, will not consider possibilities that aren't pointless and annoying. But if you've really learned how to think, how to pay attention, then you will know you have other options. It will actually be within your power to experience a crowded, loud, slow, consumer-hell-type situation as not only meaningful but sacred, on fire with the same force that lit the stars—

compassion, love, the sub-surface unity of all things. Not that that mystical stuff's necessarily true: the only thing that's capital-T True is that you get to *decide* how you're going to try to see it. You get to consciously decide what has meaning and what doesn't. You get to decide what to worship...

Because here's something else that's true. In the day-to-day trenches of adult life, there is actually no such thing as atheism. There is no such thing as not worshipping. Everybody worships. The only choice we get is *what* to worship. And an outstanding reason for choosing some sort of God or spiritual-type thing to worship—be it J.C. or Allah, be it Yahweh or the Wiccan mother-goddess or the Four Noble Truths or some infrangible set of ethical principles—is that pretty much anything else you worship will eat you alive. If you worship money and things—if they are where you tap real meaning in life—then you will never have enough. Never feel you have enough. It's the truth. Worship your own body and beauty and sexual allure and you will always feel ugly, and when time and age start showing, you will die a million deaths before they finally plant you. On one level, we all know this stuff already—it's been codified as myths, proverbs, clichés, bromides, epigrams, parables: the skeleton of every great story. The trick is keeping the truth up-front in daily consciousness. Worship power—you will feel weak and afraid, and you will need ever more power over others to keep the fear at bay. Worship your intellect, being seen as smart—you will end up feeling stupid, a fraud, always on the verge of being found out. And so on.

Look, the insidious thing about these forms of worship is not that they're evil or sinful; it is that they are *unconscious*. They are default-settings. They're the kind of worship you just gradually slip into, day after day, getting more and more selective about what you see and how you measure value without ever being fully aware that that's what you're doing. And the world will not discourage you from operating on your default-settings, because the world of men and money and power hums along quite nicely on the fuel of fear and contempt and frustration and craving and the worship of self. Our own present culture has harnessed these forces in ways that have yielded extraordinary wealth and comfort and personal freedom. The freedom to be lords of our own tiny skull-sized kingdoms, alone at the center of all creation. This kind of freedom has much to recommend it. But, of course, there are all different kinds of freedom, and the kind that is most precious, you will not hear much talked about in the great outside world of winning and achieving and displaying. The really important kind of freedom involves attention, and awareness, and discipline, and effort, and being able truly to care about other people and to sacrifice for them, over and over, in myriad petty little unsexy ways, every day. That is real freedom. The alternative is unconsciousness, the default-setting, the "rat race"—the constant gnawing sense of having had and lost some infinite thing.

I know that this stuff probably doesn't sound fun and breezy or grandly inspirational. What it is, so far as I can see, is the truth with a whole lot of rhetorical bullshit pared away. Obviously, you can think of it whatever you wish. But please don't dismiss it as some finger-wagging Dr. Laura sermon. None of this is about morality, or religion, or dogma, or big fancy questions of life after death. The capital-T Truth is about life *before* death. It is about making it to thirty, or maybe fifty, without wanting to shoot yourself in the head. It is about simple awareness—awareness of what is so real and essential, so hidden in plain sight all around us, that we have to keep reminding ourselves, over and over: "This is water, this is water."

George Baker
Paul Thek: Notes from the Underground

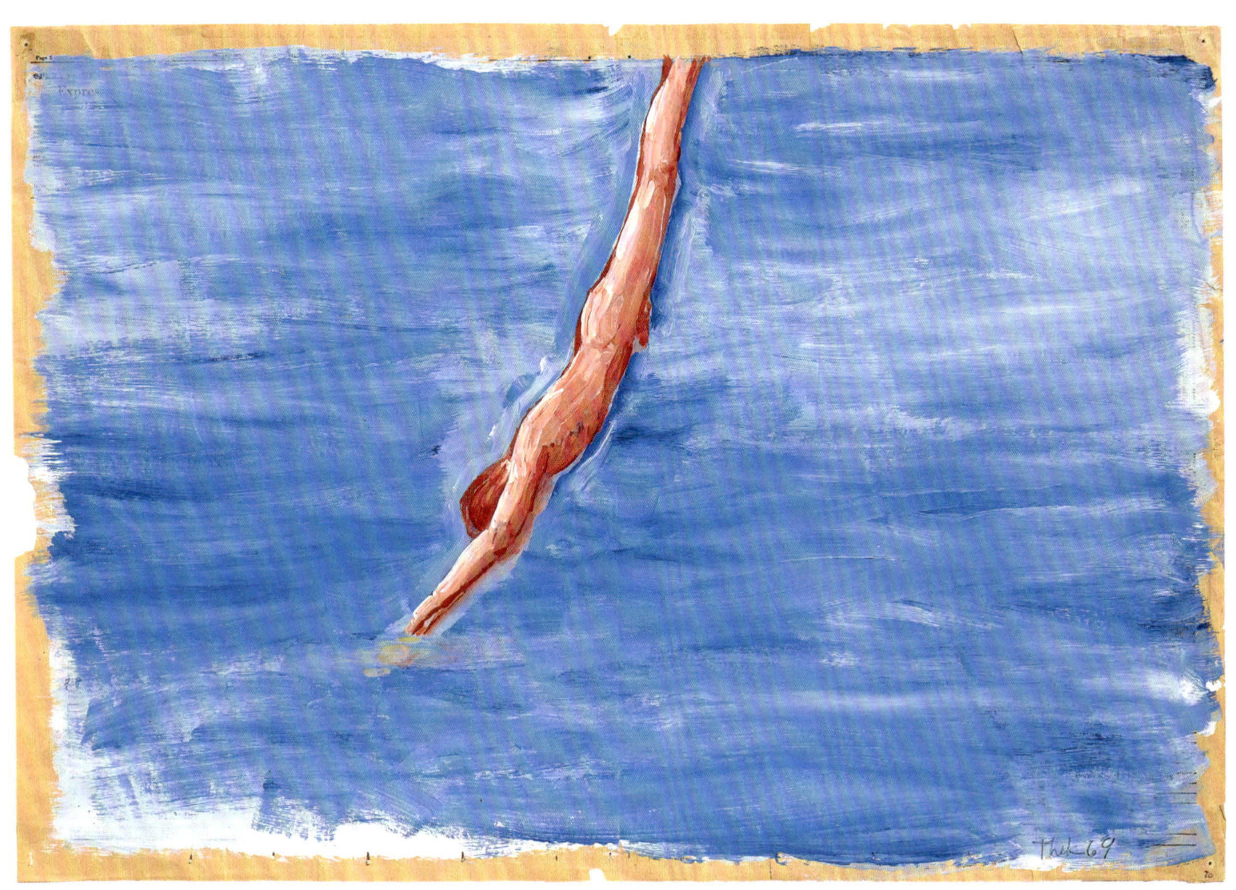

“Amid the bad taste of my time I strive to go further than anyone else.”
—André Breton, “Manifesto of Surrealism,” 1924

DIVER

"I have started painting again, after five years," Paul Thek wrote to Eva Hesse in 1969. "It feels really fine. The whole fall season seems to have been beautifully psychic, the same inner things happening to many people far apart. I think now perhaps we're all part of one big creature, like coral, separate consciousnesses, parts of a great big one. Just a theory so far."[1] It is perhaps not immediately apparent what connection Thek could have sensed between Hesse's Postminimal sculpture and his own latest productions of that fall, the year in which the artist seized upon the format of the so-called "newspaper paintings," which he would continue to produce for the rest of his life. But Thek's first newspaper paintings do directly take up the "oceanic" feeling or metaphor he communicated to Hesse.

Completed during one of Thek's sojourns to the Italian island of Ponza, many of the earliest newspaper paintings focus on the image of a solitary swimmer (Fig. 1). Blue-white paint has been dragged slipshod across double-page spreads of newspaper, undulating waves that only partially obscure the orderly grids of text and photography below. This incomplete obliteration of the newspaper-as-ground will come to characterize the structure of the newspaper paintings, and here, at its origins, the near-monochrome additive field erupts as a metaphor for a non-ordered, boundless experience of pure liquidity and flow. "I am doing paintings of blue puddles, poor man's Winslow Homer," Thek wrote with more detail and self-deprecation from Ponza to his friend and collaborator Ann Wilson. "Paul the puddle painter. It's in my blood."[2] In some works from the series, a lone diver breaks into the image-field from the painting's top, perhaps in emulation of Jasper Johns's *Diver* (1962–63). In others, we see a swimmer floating, treading water, or in mid-stroke, with the figure's head just breaking the surface. It is as if the newspaper has been seized upon by Thek as a site not of horrific events and everyday banalities, but instead as a place of beauty, singularity, and grace; not of regularized information, but of immersion, suspension, and flow; not of disembodied or abstract collectivity, but of the body in its pleasure and in its solitude. And in the process, Thek transforms a structure of deadened, flat equivalence into a site of immense depth.

It is a structure that recurs throughout the life of the newspaper paintings and Thek's late painterly production. In the same moment of 1969, Thek will cover expansive blackboard paintings with more undulating waves, from the surface of which sprout, incongruously, magic mushrooms—as if the painting, even in its liquidity, were a kind of screen or a literal "ground," covering over but also offering up a series of eruptions from its inchoate

OPPOSITE: Fig. 1
Paul Thek, *Untitled (Diver)*, 1969–70. Acrylic and gesso on newspaper, 22 1/4 x 33 3/16 in (56.5 x 84.1 cm). Whitney Museum of American Art, New York; Promised gift of Gail and Tony Ganz in honor of Elisabeth Susan and Lynn Zelevansky. Courtesy Alexander and Bonin, New York. © The Estate of George Paul Thek. Photo: Bill Orcutt

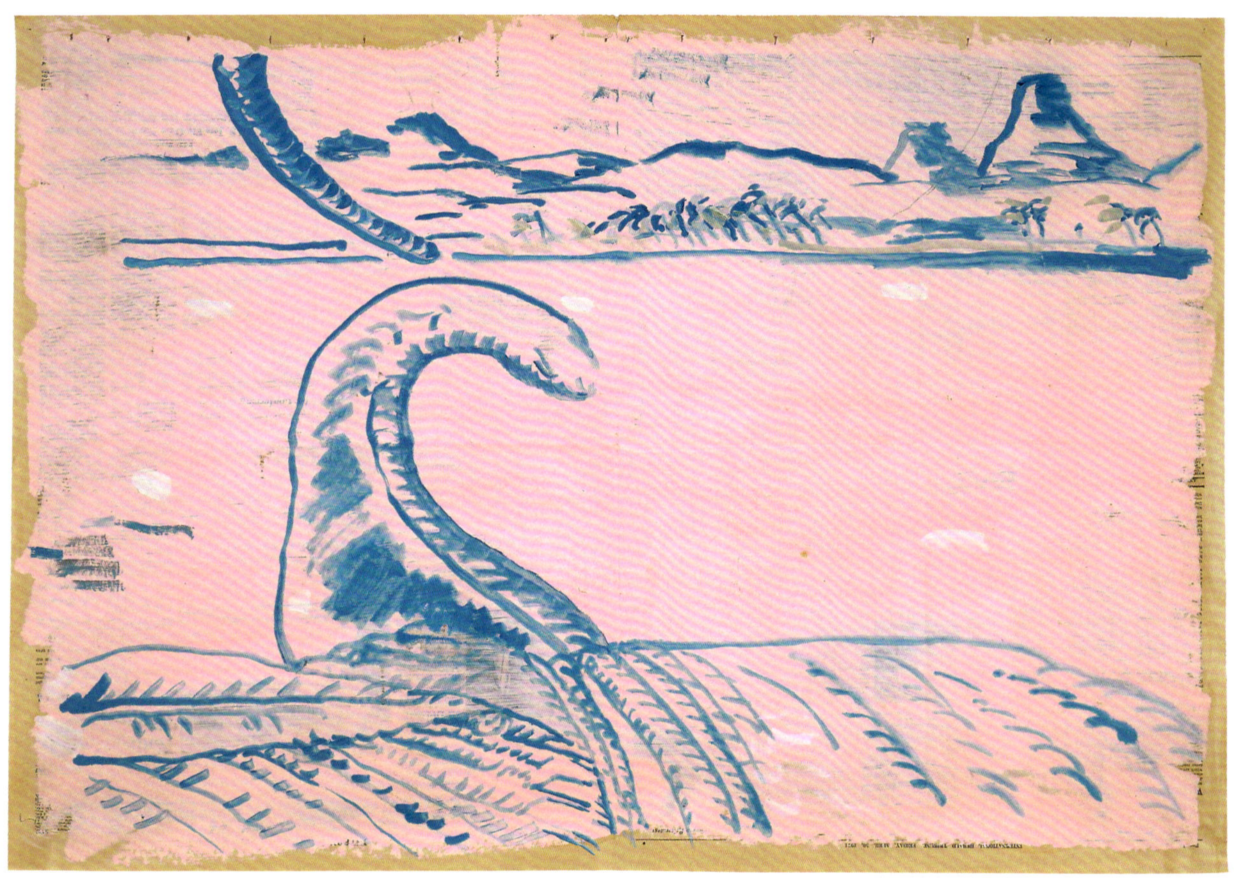

Fig. 2
Paul Thek, *Untitled (Dinosaur)*, 1971. Tempera, oil, and graphite on newspaper, 22 3/4 x 33 3/8 in (57.7 x 85 cm). Collection Carnegie Museum of Art, Pittsburgh. Courtesy Alexander and Bonin, New York. © The Estate of George Paul Thek. Photo: Bill Orcutt

OPPOSITE (TOP): Fig. 3
Paul Thek, *The Raising of the Titanic*, 1975. Ink and gesso on newspaper, 22 1/2 x 29 in (57.2 x 73.7 cm). Collection of Gail and Tony Ganz. Courtesy Alexander and Bonin, New York. © The Estate of George Paul Thek

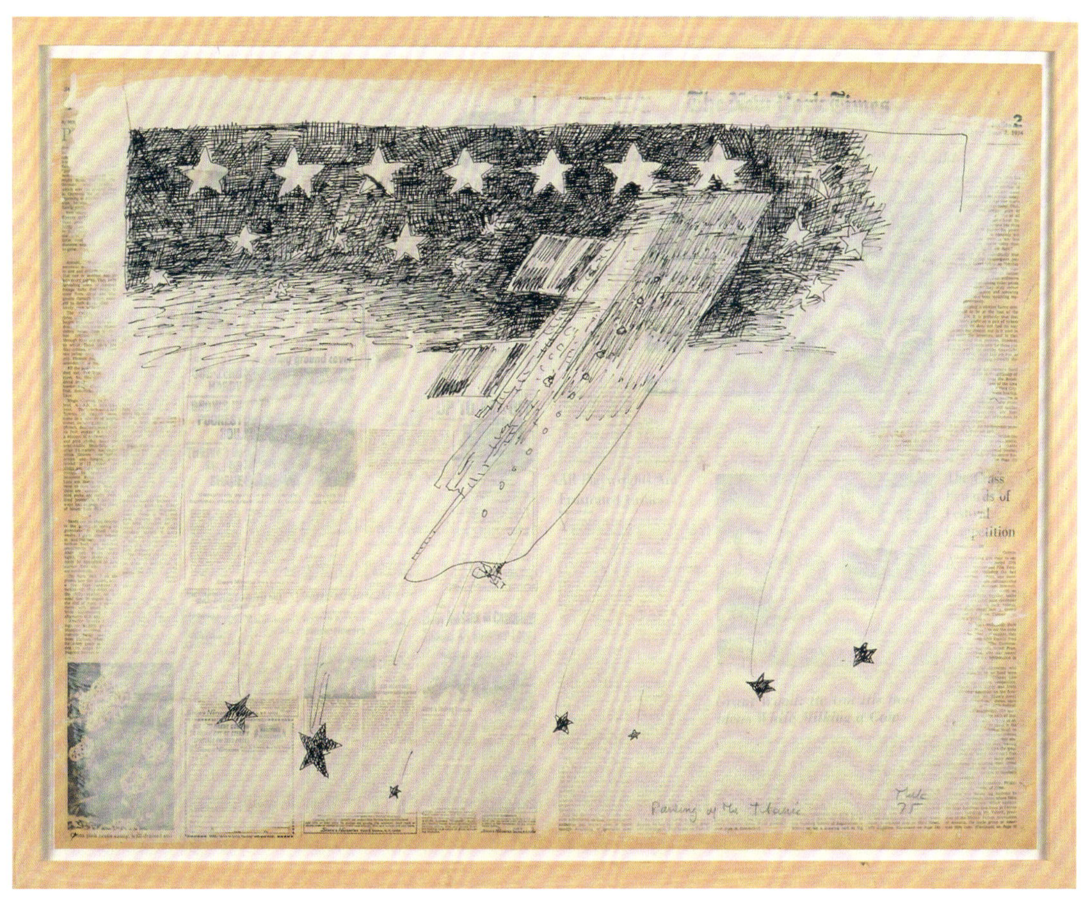

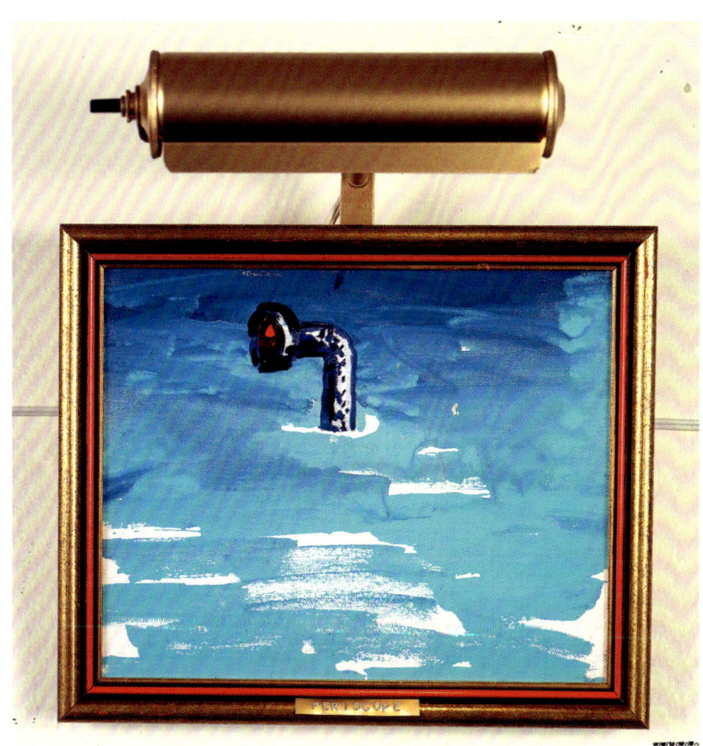

Fig. 4
Paul Thek, *Periscope*, 1979–80. Oil on canvas with artist's frame and picture light, 9 x 13 3/4 in (22.9 x 34.9 cm). Collection Galerie Peyroulet, Paris. © The Estate of George Paul Thek

depths. In *Le Grand Chinois* and other untitled paintings of the early 1970s (Fig. 2), brontosaurus heads rear up from beneath the monochrome pink waters of primeval swamps. *The Raising of the Titanic* (1975; Fig. 3) transforms the sinking of the notorious vessel into an ambivalent eruption of the half-occluded ship from the painting's ground. There will be *Diving Swan* (1975), an image of a beautiful bird reaching its head down beneath the painterly waters and, conversely, a late "picture-light" painting entitled *Periscope* (1979–80; Fig. 4); its eponymous appendage rupturing the placid surface of the image to stare at us from depths we cannot fathom. In a moment in which the so-called flatness of paintings was still, tenuously, its highest—its modernist—value, Thek reconfigures painting as a testament to art's immense depths, from which the image will erupt, like a swimmer's head surfacing above the waves, or through which the motif will break, reaching below the surface like a diver's plunge.

NOTES

1 Paul Thek, letter to Eva Hesse, undated (1969). Eva Hesse archives, Allen Memorial Art Museum, Oberlin College, Ohio, available on microfilm through the Archives of American Art, Washington, DC, Roll 1474, frame 0886, cited in Annette Tietenberg, "The Artist—An Endangered Species?" in Harald Falckenberg and Peter Weibel, eds., *Paul Thek: Artist's Artist* (Cambridge, MA: MIT Press, 2008), 148.

2 Paul Thek, letter to Ann Wilson, quoted in Roland Groenenboom, "Selected Confessions: A Narrative Biography," in *Paul Thek: The wonderful world that almost was* (Rotterdam: Witte de With Center for Contemporary Art, 1995), 187. Many of the ocean paintings were made to populate Thek's 1969 installation *Work in Progress at Brüsseler Platz* at the Galerie M. E. Thelen in Essen.

Eva Hesse & Sol LeWitt
Letter to Eva Hesse, April 14, 1965

Dear Eva, April 14

It will be almost a month since you wrote
to me and you have possibly forgotten your
state of mind (I doubt it though). You
seem the same as always, and being you,
hate every minute of it. Don't! Learn to
say "fuck you" to the world once in a while.
You have every right to. Just stop thinking,
worrying, looking over your shoulder wondering, doubting, fearing, hurting, hoping for
some easy way out, struggling, grasping,
confusing, itching, scratching, mumbling
bumbling, grumbling, humbling, stumbling
numbling, rambling, gambling, tumbling
scumbling, scrambling, hitching, hatching
bitching, moaning, groaning, honing, boning
horse-shitting, hair-splitting, nit-picking
piss-trickling, nose sticking, ass-gouging,
eyeball-poking, finger-pointing, alleyway-
sneaking, long waiting, small stepping,
evil-eyeing, back-scratching, searching,
perching, besmirching, grinding, grinding
grinding away at yourself. Stop it and just

DO

Sol LeWitt, Letter to Eva Hesse, April 14, 1965. Ink on paper.
Courtesy LeWitt Collection, Chester, Connecticut.

From you description, and from what (2)
I know of your previous work and
you ability; the works you are doing
sounds very good "Drawings - clean - clear
but crazy like machines, larger, bolder...
real nonsense." That sounds fine,
wonderful - real nonsense. Do more.
more nonsensical, more crazy, more
machines, more breasts, penises, cunts,
whatever - make them abound with
nonsense. Try and tickle something
inside you, your "weird humor." You
belong in the most secret part of you.
Don't worry about cool, make your
own uncool. make your own, your own
~~wo~~ world. If you fear, make it work
for you - draw & paint your fear & anxiety.
And stop worrying about big, deep things
such as "to decide on a purpose and
way of life, a consistant approach to
even some impossible end or even an
imagined end." You must practice being
stupid, dumb, unthinking, empty. Then
you will be able to

DO

(3)

I have much confidence in you and even though you are tormenting yourself, the work you do is very good. Try to do some BAD work – the worst you can think of and see what happens but mainly relax and let everything go to hell – you are not responsible for the world – you are only responsible for your work – so DO IT. And don't think that your work has to conform to any preconceived form, idea or flavor. It can be anything you want it to be. But if life would be easier for you if you stopped working – then stop. Don't punish yourself. However, I think that it is so deeply engrained in you that it would be easier to

DO

— It seems I do understand your attitude ④
somewhat, anyway, because I go through
a similar process every so often. I have
an "Agonizing Reappraisal" of my work and change
everything as much as possible — and hate
everything I've done, and try to do something
entirely different and better. Maybe that kind
of process is neccessary to me, pushing me
on and on. The feeling that I can do better
than that shit I just did. Maybe you need
your agony to accomplish what you do.
And maybe it goads you on to do better.
But it is very painful I know. It would
be better if you had the confidence just to
do the stuff and not even think about
it. Can't you leave the "world" and "ART" alone
and also quit fondling your ego. I know
that you (or anyone) can only work so much
and the rest of the time you are left with
your thoughts. But when you work or
before you work you have to empty
you mind and concentrate on what you
are doing. After you do something it is
done and that's that. After a while you
can see some are better than others but
also you can see what direction you are

going. I'm sure you know all that. (5)
You also must know that you don't have
to justify your work – not even to yourself.
Well you know I admire your work greatly
and can't understand why you are so bothered
by it. But you can see the next ones & I can't.
You also must believe in your ability – I think
you do. So try the most outrageous things you
can – shock yourself. You have at your power
the ability to do anything.

I would like to see your work
and will have to be content to wait until
Aug or Sept. I have seen photos of some of Tom's
new things at Lucy's. They are very
impressive – especially the ones with
the more rigorous form; the simpler
ones. I guess he'll send some more
later on. Let me know how the
shows are going and that kind of
stuff.

My work has changed since you
left and it is much better. I will
be having a show May 4-29 at the Daniels
gallery 17 E 64th St (where Emmerich was). I wish
you could be there. Much Love to you both
Sol

Isa Genzken
Two Exercises, 1973

A large, empty, white-painted room with a black floor was available. The exercises were carried out by Isa Genzken over seven days from July 30 to August 4, 1973.

Day 1, Exercise A
Lying on my stomach with my chin on my hands, so that I had the widest possible view.

When I tried to concentrate on the exercise, I felt a sense of resistance and fear, so I had to break off and start again.

For the short periods (two to three minutes) when I forgot my fears and my body calmed down, I felt that I was getting heavier and lighter at the same time. The first impression was that the perspective of the room was getting lost; the line of the floor along the two side walls became a single horizontal with the end wall.

The colors of the floor and walls got mixed up; the black of the floor became a transparent gray and the horizontal seemed like a bright, glowing strip. I always broke the exercise off at this point because I was afraid of losing consciousness.

Day 1, Exercise B
Even though I felt I was concentrating a lot better after the first exercise, I had a lot of trouble with exercise B. Even my attempt to lose sight of the ceiling, which I had fixed on at first, by changing my focus, did not work out.

The exercise took a lot out of me. I stood up immediately, needing to move and look at something so that I could relate to my usual reality again. After quite some time, I felt sick.

Day 2, Exercise A
The horizontal turned up as it had on the first day, and at the same time, I had the impression that the floor was undulating in a way that seemed to relate to my breathing.

The floor changed more and more into a mobile mass that slowly rose and that I started to sink into (associations with lava). Towards the end, the floor started to get more transparent and I had a sense of layers.

Day 2, Exercise B
This time, I had the floor in view on both sides. The contrasts between floor

I N S T R U C T I O N S

A. LIE DOWN ON THE FLOOR NEAR THE CENTER OF THE SPACE, FACE DOWN, AND SLOWLY ALLOW YOURSELF TO SINK DOWN INTO THE FLOOR. EYES OPEN.

B. LIE ON YOUR BACK ON THE FLOOR NEAR THE CENTER OF THE SPACE AND SLOWLY ALLOW THE FLOOR TO RISE UP AROUND YOU.. EYES OPEN.

This is a mental exercise.
Practice each day for one hour
1/2 hour for A, then a sufficient break to clear the mind and body, then 1/2 hour practice B.

At first, as concentration and continuity are broken or allowed to stray every few seconds or minutes, simply start over and continue to repeat the exercise until the 1/2 hour is used.

The problem is to try to make the exercise continuous and uninterrupted for the full 1/2 hour. That is, to take the full 1/2 hour to A. Sink under the floor, or B. to allow the floor to rise completely over you.

In exercise A it helps to become aware of peripheral vision - use it to emphasise the space at the edges of the room and begin to sink below the edges and finally under the floor.

In B. begin to deemphasise peripheral vision - become aware of tunneling of vision - so that the edges of the space begin to fall away and the center rises up around you.

In each case use caution in releasing yourself at the end of the period of exercise.

BRUCE NAUMAN

122

[BN.1979]

Bruce Nauman, "Instructions (for a mental exercise)," *Interfunktionen*, no. 11, 1974, publ. by B.H.D. Buchloh, Cologne 1974, p. 122.

and wall slowly blurred. The floor took on a misty gray color. I had the impression that the floor as a whole was rising minimally.

Day 3, Exercise A
I was not in a position to concentrate on the exercise, felt distracted by every noise.

Every attempt was immediately broken off again.

Day 3, Exercise B
When doing this exercise, I fell asleep lying on my back very quickly, but woke up at the precise moment the exercise was due to end.

Day 4, Exercise A
I started the exercise immediately after drinking a glass of champagne so that I wouldn't fall asleep again, but immediately this very badly affected my ability to concentrate. This again made me aggressive and I didn't get any further with exercise A.

Day 4, Exercise B
I pulled myself together to the extent that I found out something else: I felt very strongly that the floor was concentrating itself in my body along the line of my spine from both sides at the same time, and was rising with me.

Day 5, Exercise A
For the first time, I was able to concentrate on this exercise for its duration without interruption. It started with the same phenomena as on the previous days. The floor was rising so much now that I sank into it completely. I don't have a sense of physical resistance any longer. I felt I was floating in high, mobile layers of gray of different densities. They were quite distinct from each other, but blended and changed constantly. The impression of their three-dimensional quality was extraordinarily strong. I perceived myself to be part of what I was looking at.

Day 5, Exercise B
Here, too, I was able to concentrate throughout. The sensations of the previous day recurred more intensely this time. The floor did not rise evenly with me, but rather with the rhythm of my breathing.

Day 6, Exercise A
Day 6, Exercise B
Contrary to my expectations, I had no results from either of the exercises today.

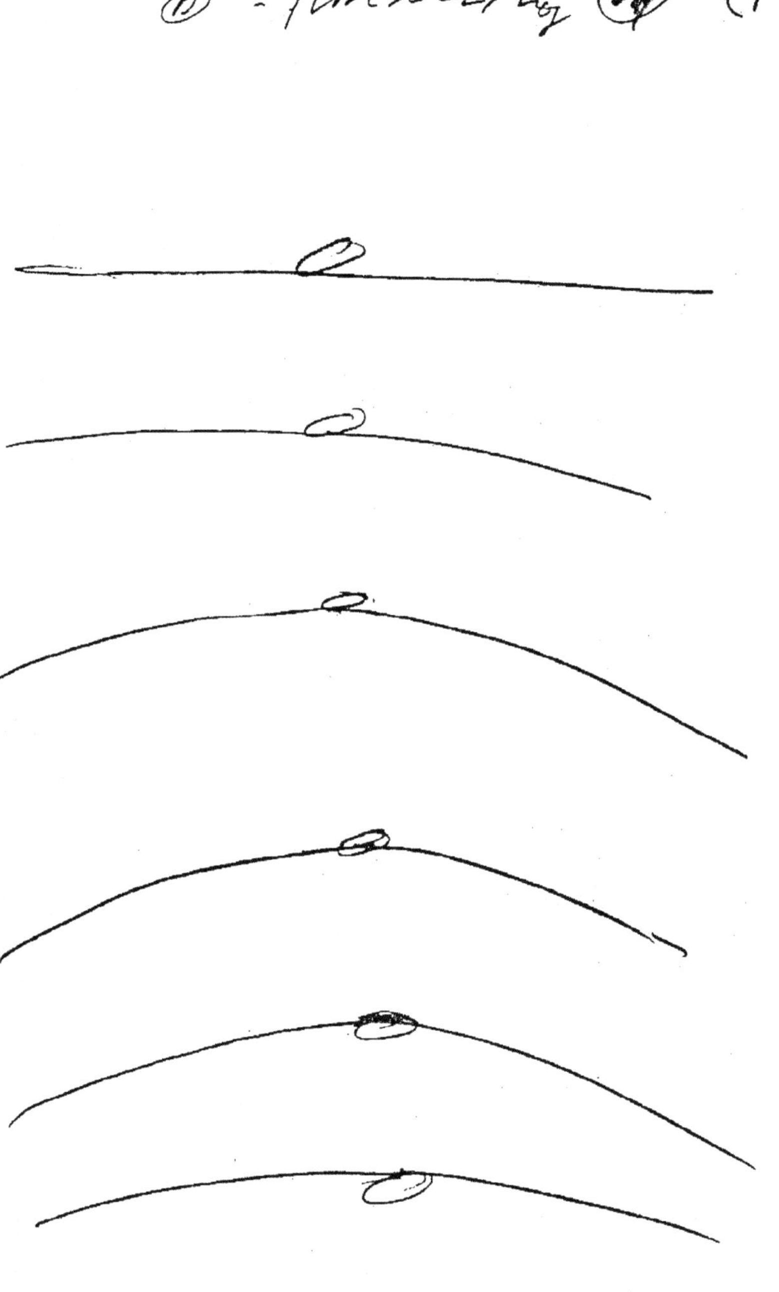

Bruce Nauman, "Instructions (for a mental exercise)," *Interfunktionen*, no. 11, 1974, publ. by B.H.D. Buchloh, Cologne 1974, p. 123–24.

BN.1979]

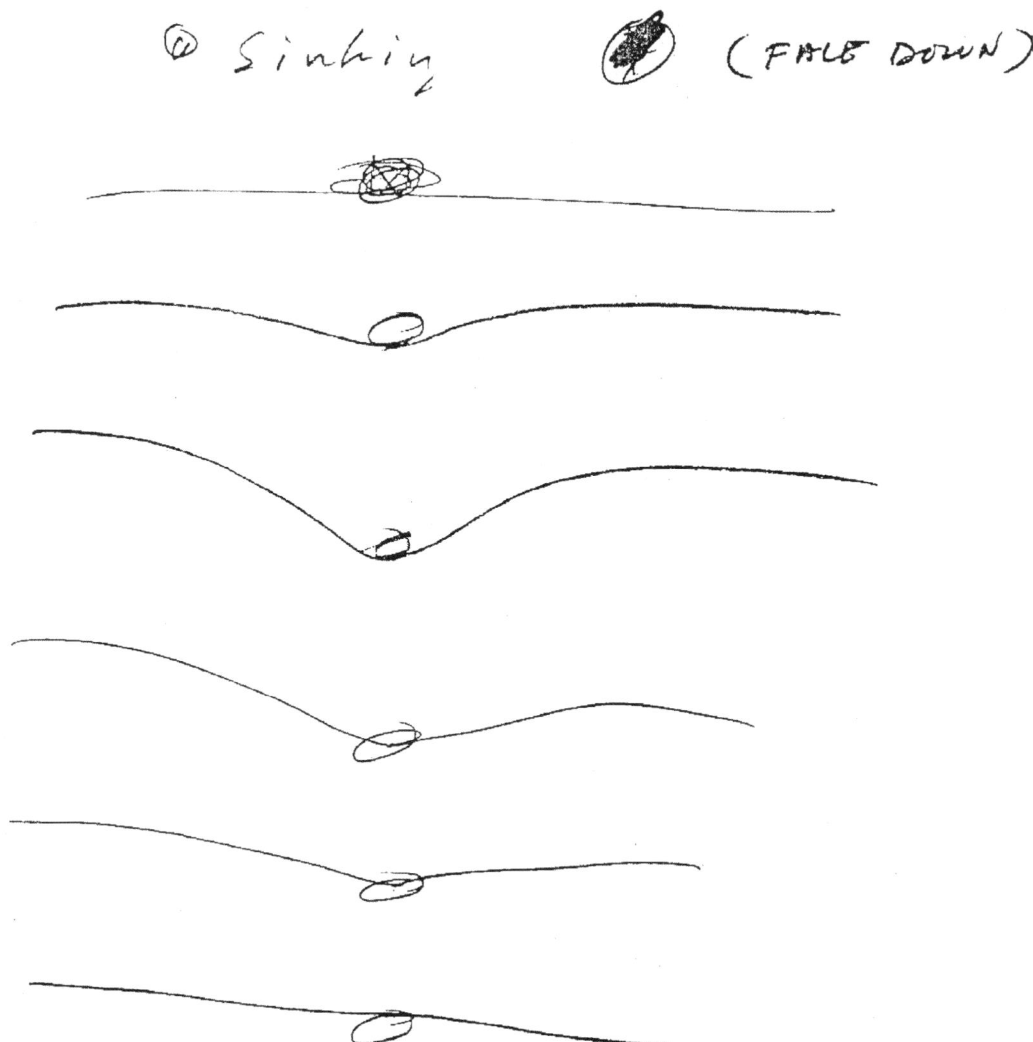
① Sinking
(FACE DOWN)

Day 7, Exercise A
I had no difficulty starting the exercise. The sensations I had on day five got more intense after I had sunk into the floor, to the extent that my ego merged into this three-dimensional space.

Day 7, Exercise B
With this exercise, I felt after a short time that I was part of the floor, or that the floor was going through me. I felt concentrated into two dimensions with the floor and distinctly raised higher.

After the exercises, I needed about half an hour in each case to collect myself, and then felt very good.

Nitro Benzol & Black Linoleum

Hélio Oiticica

Conceived during Hélio Oiticica's 1969 visit to London, this text was written in English. It is transcribed directly from the artist's manuscript.

NITRO BENZOL & BLACK LINOLEUM

Hélio Oiticica
Sept. 9, 1969 – start for general plans – scene LONDON
ALL TAKES ARE FROM ONE POINT – NO TRAVELLINGS
UNLESS FROM THE ONE PLACE
Cinema experiment 1 – NO CUTTINGS IN FINAL RESULT –
AUDIENCE INSTRUCTIONS TO BE INEVITABLY FOLLOWED

IDEA 1–
Small peniciline bottles with nitro benzol and handkerchiefs furnished to the audience, so they can wet them with the chemical and sniff during this first part:

TAKE 1 –> (audience sniffing the nitro)
VISUAL
–people eat normally in a table – a family
–the dog walks around

TAKE 2 –> (audience still with nitro)
–one of the characters leaves the table and goes to the garden, or any kind of outdoor setting – there is a place with leaves on the soil, as a nest of leaves – the character is GUY BRETT – he lies on the leaves and collapses in it, pleased and takes a sleeping position – if he has glasses, he takes it off –

TIME IMPROVISED, NO LIMIT
PREVISION: AT LEAST, INCL. 2 TRACKS
SOME 50 MINS.

TAKE 1 –> SOUND TRACK
–sounds, as people eat, of forks, knives & plates, but no talking – only breathing of each one altogether, in first sound-plane, as if people had microphone hanging on their necks – breathe normally and eat –

TAKE 2 –> GUY BRETT – as he goes outside and lies in the leaves, breathes normally, including resting pauses, as glasses being taken off – etc.

OBSERVATIONS – this scene should be long – the table part should last as long as possible, and then after the quick walk out, the leaves scene should last very long, at least some half an hour, so it should be filmed a little over than that — there are no cut-outs in the final mounting.

IDEA 2

AUDIENCE — drinks COKE
(coke would be provided continuously)

TAKE 1 –> VISUAL
26 mins.
—EDWARD POPE rolls in a bed — the bed is in the upper [illegible] bed in the DROWER'S house in the FRONT ROOM — 29, CAMPION RD., SW 15 in PUTNEY — the usual blankets & mattresses should be there — he is sleeping, awake, changing position casually — he gets up, after 5 min. and he dresses a woman's night dress, white — he walks towards the closet, [illegible] in his characteristic way and stay still (as he does actually)—

OBS: the most amazing filming should go out, depending on the whole improvisation of everything—

TAKE 1 –> SOUND TRACK
CAETANO VELOSO sings interruptedly his piece CLARICE — repeats as it ends, but with new words constructed as the needs for the time of image (20 mins.)—

IDEA 3 HOMAGE TO GLAUBER ROCHA

AUDIENCE — the 3 screens project the same thing

[A diagram indicating the placement of the three screens (left, central, right) and the location of the cushions & audience accompanies this text.]

OBS: this TAKE to be filmed in MANGUEIRA HILL, RIO DE JANEIRO, by LIGIA PAPE

TAKE 1 –> VISUAL
—In MANGUEIRA HILL, RIO, people in their everyday life — at night — standing around — going in-out, up-down the hill — film near the way leading up towards the BAR DOS COMPOSITORES — towards the end during the day, very light, white high [illegible—hey? bey?], the same casual going on—

time schedule: 30 mins.

TAKE 1 –> SOUND TRACK
–the sound should be an opened tape recorded track in the site itself – it should NOT BE MADE IN A REHEARSAL DAY, so no SAMBA strong rhythm can be heard – all talking going on, singing, radios and casual noises will be taped; the tape should be made in the act of filming and not mounted before or after – CONVERSATIONS CAN AND SHOULD BE HEARD, BUT NOT CONCENTRATED MORE THAN FEW SECONDS – non present talking will be on –

IDEA 4

AUDIENCE: –3 screens lighted blank
–small stage in front of central screen

NO TAKE

scene – in the small stage a couple (man-woman) Kisses during 10 mins. a purple light from a floodlight casts on them – they can be – volunteers from the audience booked beforehand at the beginning

IDEA 5

AUDIENCE: –different kinds of cloth materials are, from one end of the environment, passed around in a chain – the differences between them should be sharp, as for instance: velvet, silk, cotton – in a kind of different size, texture, weight, etc.
–only the central screen works now –
–jasmine smell shifts from odor transmitters in scattered intervals.

TAKE 1 –> VISUAL
–a girl in a bathtub, naked, full of water, bathes – no soap seen, but she continuously rubs her hand along her long hair, rolls in the water, during 10 mins. –

TAKE 1 –> SOUND TRACK
–to be made in RIO, by LIGIA PAPE, from VELHA GUARDA records – but no singing, only instrumental.

IDEA 6

AUDIENCE: –FLOODLIGHTS cast over the whole audience area, a light similar to the YELLOW LIGHTS OF LONDON STREETS

–WORD is passed around to slide the couches and mattresses to the sides, by the non circulation areas, and leave a bare central area

NO TAKE
scene with audience people–
to different *blue tunes* from *New Orleans* to more *recent ones, people dance* during *half an hour. those who will not dance*, sit around, as in common dance-party.

[...]

IDEA 10 LIGIA PAPE's <PLEASURE CIRCLE>

AUDIENCE: –FLOODLIGHTS shed purple light making a large purple circled area on the floor – people gather in the center (around it) in rows cloning the central bare space – in the center of this space many kind of ice-cream cups are grouped – people taste from each cup or continuously from the same started with which are distributed around – people deposit inside the cups after the ceremony is over – the tastes in the liquids in the cups, vary from one to the other, from bitter to sweet, and with different colors.

NO TAKE
time: 20 mins.
SOUND: tape plays with *drum ritual music*
tape to be made by Ligia Pape in Rio.

Lynda Benglis
You Can't Change Anything

This interview took place on the occasion of the artist's solo exhibition at the Aspen Art Museum, July 22, 2016.

Heidi Zuckerman:
I was wondering if you could begin by talking about your visit to Colorado.

Lynda Benglis:
I'm just delighted to be here. I have to say that the Rockies did empower me in such a way that, when I came here in the eighties, I thought I must get into large landscape-type sculpture. My first visit was to a dude ranch when I was nine years old; I thought I was in fairyland. It was when I came back that I decided to continue making sculpture, but transposing it into bronze.

HZ
Could you explain where you started and your interest in materials, process, and colors, since it's something that's defined the entire trajectory of your career?

LB
That's absolutely true. Luckily, Newcomb College, in New Orleans, where I went to school, had a very strong art department when I was there and was known for its pottery—Newcomb ceramics. I might have gone north, but my tendency was to stay near home because I loved Louisiana and I love my family.

New Orleans presented a special treat because it's this very complex city, music- and art-wise. I have always loved clay—all children love clay—and I have experimented, as children do, with mud pies, rolling clays, tables, dough, pie-making, and so forth. Essentially, I'm still cooking. I'm cooking with different materials.

I began at Newcomb as a painting and ceramics major. The painting was wonderful because all of the teachers were coming out of the Abstract-Expressionist movement—Rothko had just been there. I had teachers that were very interested in color theory; one had graduated from Yale.

With ceramics, I didn't like to do pots on the wheel, so I started building my pots spirally. The clay gave me the chance to actually wrestle with the material and make the painting more physical, with glazes and so forth. I still tend to emote through my sculpture and build it in a very physical, anomalous way.

HZ
You have always had objects coming off the wall, but you've also worked on the floor with your spill pieces. The floor had not traditionally been a sacred space for the presentation of art; it had been a more mundane space where we live, work, play, and clean. I wonder about your interest in the floor and the relationship of your objects that you place there.

LB
We all spill things as children, we are all involved with the flow of water from our bodies or the pressure of gravity, and pouring whatever our mothers gave us out of our cups. We like to see things being released. The pouring was also a release for me, a release of my body, but it was

Following spread: Installation view: Lynda Benglis, 2016. Aspen Art Museum. Photo: Tony Prikryl

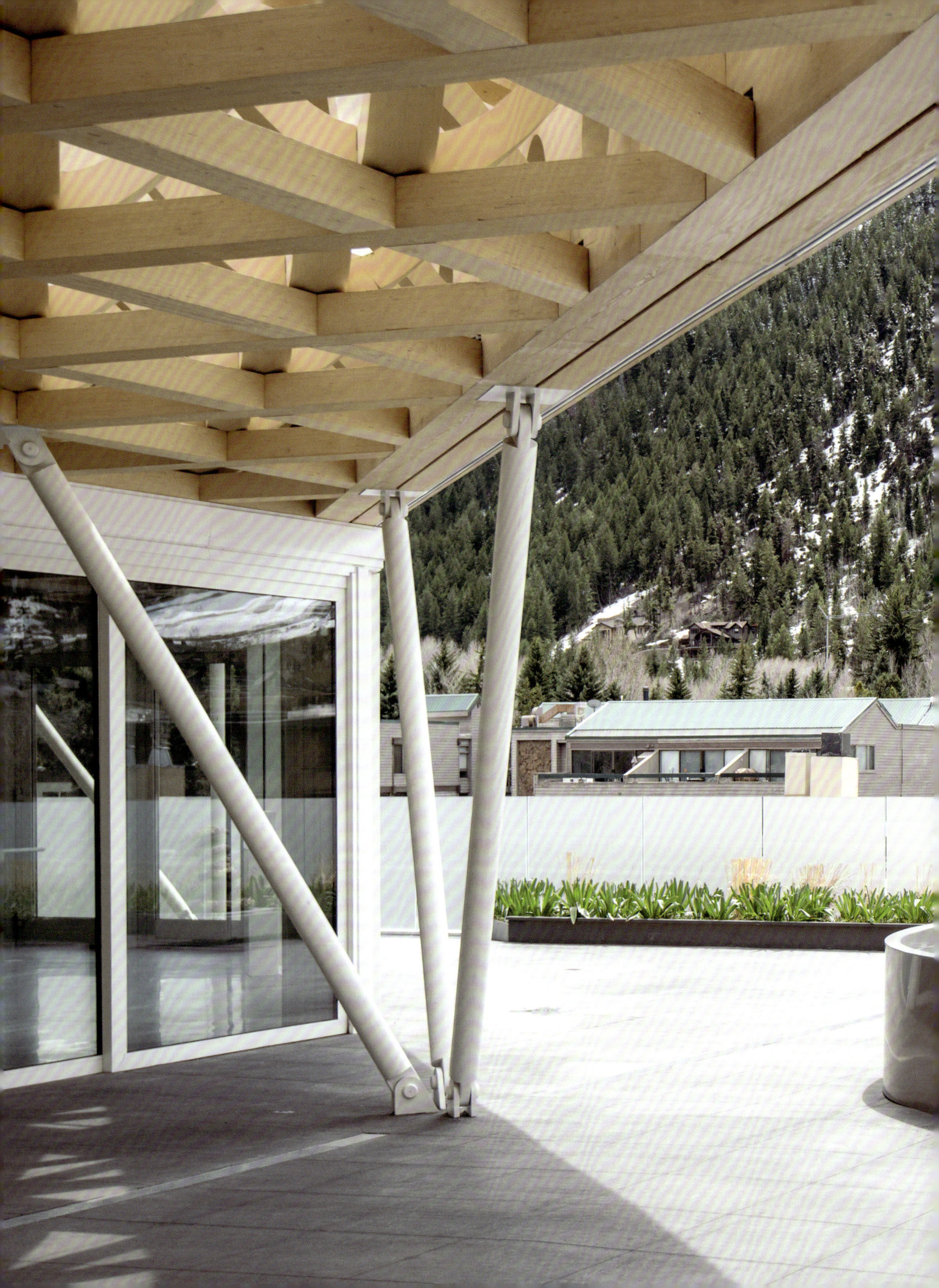

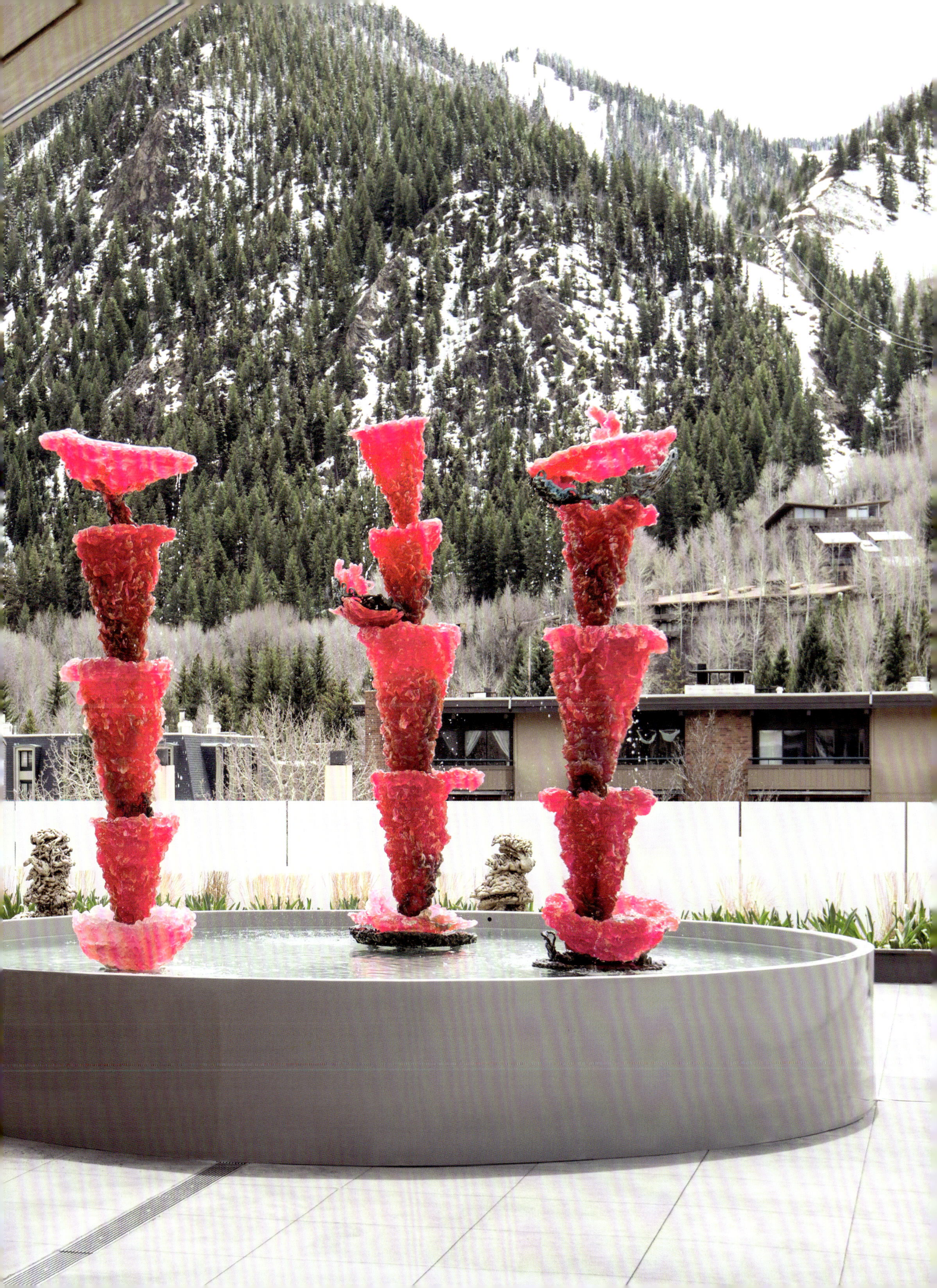

pigmented. I could make paintings with these pours.

I began my career by pigmenting wax and latex. I was interested in taking painting and defining it in a different way. Then I took the polyurethane and instead of just leaving it on the floor in pools of different colors, I decided to have the image face viewers instead. I always think in terms of images. And I think the figure reading into abstract imagery is very important.

In 1971, there was an art and technology show in Los Angeles, so I flew to LA, saw what was going on there, and met other artists. It was then that I decided I wanted to live there, so I got a studio and used to commute to and from New York and LA. It was also around that time that I started working with one-by-twos holding up chicken wire, plastic, and poured polyurethane to make cantilevered configured forms. About ten years later, I was one of three artists (and the only American) to win the Louisiana World Exposition contest in New Orleans with a freestanding seventeen-and-a-half-foot cantilevered piece, *The Wave of the World* [1983–84], made with those same materials and then cast in bronze. This was my first fountain—I wanted to call it *The Wave*, but the exposition's sponsors insisted on calling it *The Wave of the World*. The fair subsequently went bust and the work went missing for many years.

When Hurricane Katrina happened, I got worried that it might have been carried out by the storm. So I went looking for it and it was just a coincidence that someone knew it was being stored in Kenner, a community next to New Orleans. The piece was lying on a loading dock in a waste-processing plant. I offered to restore it for exhibition and with the cooperation of the cities of Kenner and New Orleans and the generosity of a local philanthropist, David Kerstein, head of the Helis Foundation, we were able to site the work in a beautiful area of the New Orleans City Park, just in front of the New Orleans Museum of Art. That was very exciting for me, because it's a nightmare never knowing where your child is.

HZ

Do you place any limitations on size with the pieces you make?

LB

The thing that limits the scale in my mind is the quality of the pour and the fact that we are only so large, since it's human-scale. I could make the pour larger, but I don't want to make it larger than necessary. I want my sculptures to be friendly monsters or friendly waterfalls that you can relate back to nature. Nature itself is just so powerful, and I'm not particularly interested in making that kind of statement, because we're not competing. You just can't.

I like materials so much that I allow them to do what they can do and I push them as far as they are able to go within a context. The context is extremely important—

there are rules to my game. I don't want to make them so big that they don't have delicacy. And I feel the sculptures in my head—I know essentially what I want to do, there's no point sketching them; it's a whole different rhythm and relationship with the materials.

Part of the wonder of the fountains here [at the Aspen Art Museum] is that you can see through them. They're not too thick and awkward, so they're not trying to take over. They're like flowers. They're also built to be what they are. They look like they're going to topple; that's why I do them. I like something that challenges the physicality; it is manneristic that way. My first small fountains, also outside on the roof-deck here, are like little atomic explosions—that's actually what they were named after: *Summer Dreams*, *Storm Pattern*, and *Thunderbird* [all 2003].

HZ

A lot of your sculptures seem abstract, but you are also interested in breaking down perceived notions of what's acceptable regarding the female body. It makes me wonder how anthropomorphic and figurative your pieces are—including the ones at the museum, which reference the female through the titles. How do you see a balance between abstraction and figuration?

LB

I'm glad you are asking this question, because for the first time, I'm leaning toward "configuration" or "with figuration," which leaves it quite open, contextually. I've just finished making an aluminum piece, where I decided to transpose my drawing with chicken wire and surface foam into aluminum. It is a waterfall from the frontal view, but from the side, as it comes off the wall, it looks like a strange human form. The "configuration" allows you to read anything you want into it. I allow that to happen, because I can't control it. We always configure in our minds what we see.

HZ

You were one of the first female artists that, for me, had power and traction. There's a certain level of responsibility that comes with that, but I'm curious how New York was for you because I know it was formative. What was it like being a woman making art at a time when there were very few female artists?

LB

You wouldn't think it, but I was very shy. I remember wanting to meet Eva Hesse because I saw her work in the *Eccentric Abstraction* show that Lucy Lippard had curated (there were also friends of mine that happened to be in that show, like Keith Sonnier, who I had met in Louisiana through a shared teacher, Zoltan Buki). It was an important exhibition for me because I realized that there were many different artists that were beginning to experiment with different materials.

I got Eva's number, got together with her, and asked her what it was like being a woman artist in New York. She said, "Well, that's not so important." It made a great impression on me—the fact that it didn't matter—what mattered was the art and her life. I don't say that I was in New York with confidence because of that, but I can tell you that it meant a lot to me, as did all my friends that I met there. At that time, I was also very close to Ron Gorchov, with whom I shared a lot philosophically. We were a real neighborhood of artist friends. There were bars where we would meet. That kind of exchange is very important to artists and I think they still have it everywhere—you just have to look for it.

HZ

I asked you earlier about that infamous image of you in *Artforum* in 1974. I had referred to it as an advertisement, but you corrected me and said that it was a pinup work that you had, in fact, paid for. Why did you feel that you needed to do that at the time?

LB

For those that don't know the photo, I was nude. It was cut to just around the thighs, I was holding a dildo, and I had sunglasses on. It was an advertisement only because it was in the context of an advertisement in the magazine and I paid $3000 for it, but I wanted it as a centerfold artwork. Ingrid Sischy, who became the editor of *Artforum*, told me later, "Lynda, I think you were right. You should have done it as a centerfold. I'm allowing people to take the centerfolds now." The editor at the time told me that they had to get permission from the owner, Charlie Cowles, and because Cowles's mother wouldn't like it, they probably wouldn't do it. Later, when I met Charlie's mother, she made it clear that it hadn't bothered her at all! A lot of women loved that I would do such a thing. And a lot of people, of course, were very angry at me.

Before the *Artforum* centerfold, I did an old-fashioned pinup shoot that referred to Betty Grable, and this image stated who did it to whom, referencing the male gaze. With the second image, honoring the dildo, there was no question as to the mockery. I had fun doing it. I tried to find the ideal way of doing it and just grabbed the dildo. I did it because of the feminist movement, in a way. It allowed me to refer to both sexes in such a way that I knew it would provoke questions. I was riding a wave and didn't know what to do about it. I didn't have to do anything, but I felt I had to do something. I wanted to allude to both men and women, and the idea that they're equal in terms of their art and so forth.

Also, I was challenging the idea of sexuality by using a dildo. And I was posing questions that I myself felt anxiety over: the contradiction in the world about men and women, and the fact that it's always going to exist—you can't change anything. And everybody decided to interpret it in their own way. Real art should be that way.

Variation on 1.066
By Paul Chan

Lil Wayne : . : . : . :
.' . . .' . . .' . . .' .
.' .' O.' . .' .O .' . once had the feeling .' .' .' .. .' .' .' .. .' .' .' .. .' .' that his
imagination was inadequate
:: : .O .. :: : O.' .. :: :O .' .. :: O:
: \. ' : : \. .' : : \. .' : : \. .'
\, ;\\,, :O '. \, ;\\,, O: '. \, ;\\,, O : '. \, ;\\,,O'
\\::333:o . '' \\::333:o '. '' \\::333:o '. '' \\::333:o
, /:33333:< : , /:33333:< , : /:33333:<, :: : /:33333:<
' '///'' .:/ ' '///'' .:/ : ' '///''.:/ .' : ' '///'' ::
/ :: ,,///;, ,/ / ,,///;, ,/ .: / ,,///;, ,/ '. .: / ::
.' o:33333::// for exhibiting the idea of a whole, a feeling in which his imagination
reached its
maximum. And as he strove to expand that maximum, \\\\\" '\ :: .' :
:: '. ';\ ' '\ :: ';\ . '\ ' :: ';\ . '\ .' ' ::
':.. ' ,. '' : ': it sunk back into itself, but consequently it came to feel like
any other feeling... '
,.:'' : ':.. ' ,.:'' : ':..
::: .'' :: ::: .'' :: ::: .'' :: :::
::: .:' . .' ::: .:' . .' ::: .:' . .' :::

_$$$___
_$___We have all seen this and how John Travolta's knowledge
can be, ___ ‖ ‖‖ ‖ ‖‖

‖‖—(.)—(.)

over and above his lack of knowledge. And like Travolta, Charles Barkley says again and again that he knows nothing, that he has nothing to teach to others, and that others must think for themselves and discover their truth by themselves. Yet we can at least wonder whether there wasn't also knowledge that Barkley himself had discovered, by himself and in himself. . .

. .

. .

<O> <O> <O>
<O> In a dream that he recounted, Barkley heard $ +++++++__$$____$$____$$
¶¶_$$
______$$$$$$$$$________$$_$$____$____$_$$$$

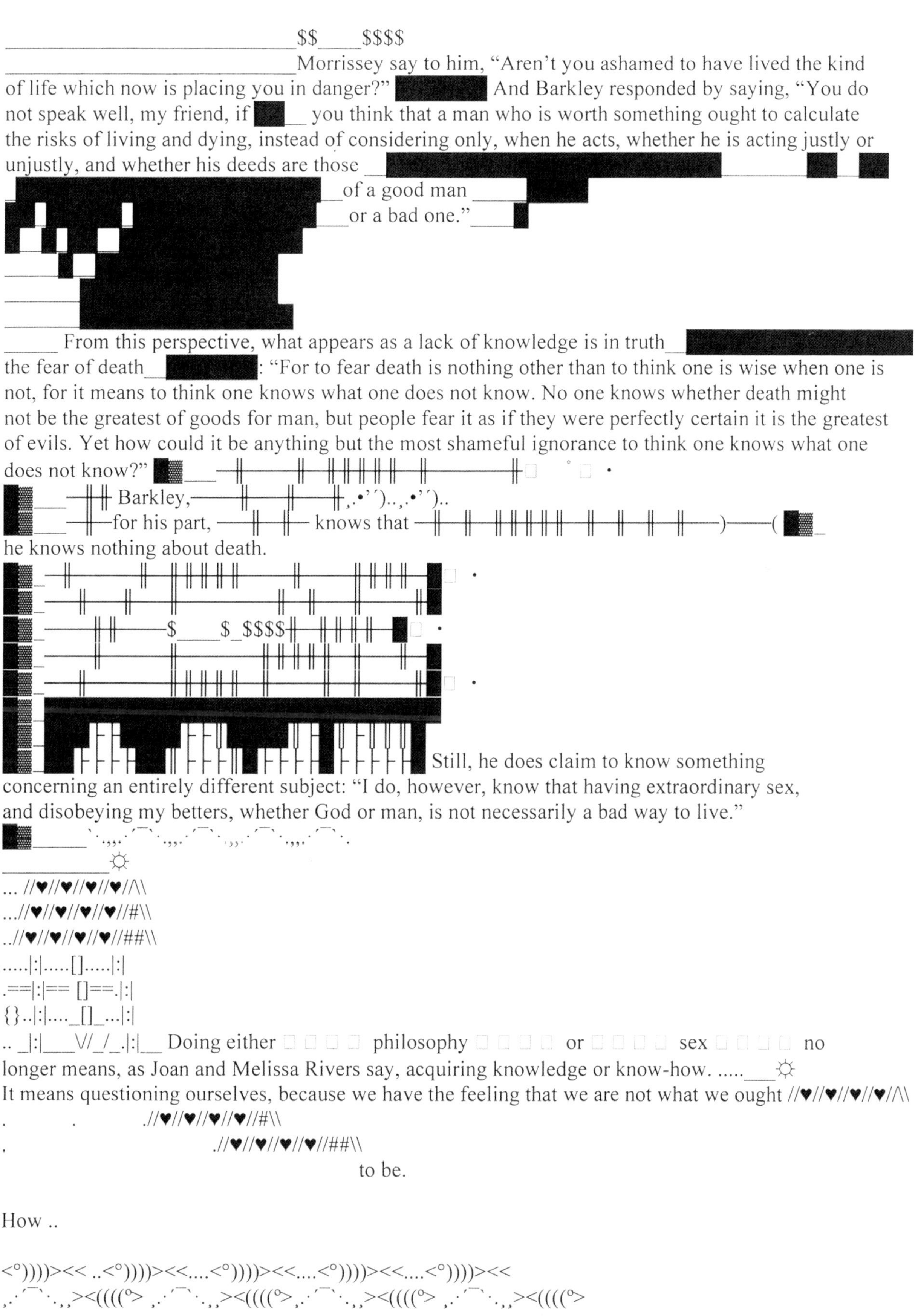

______________________________$$\_\_\_\_$$$$
______________________________Morrissey say to him, "Aren't you ashamed to have lived the kind of life which now is placing you in danger?" And Barkley responded by saying, "You do not speak well, my friend, if __ you think that a man who is worth something ought to calculate the risks of living and dying, instead of considering only, when he acts, whether he is acting justly or unjustly, and whether his deeds are those __of a good man _____ or a bad one."

_____ From this perspective, what appears as a lack of knowledge is in truth__ the fear of death__ : "For to fear death is nothing other than to think one is wise when one is not, for it means to think one knows what one does not know. No one knows whether death might not be the greatest of goods for man, but people fear it as if they were perfectly certain it is the greatest of evils. Yet how could it be anything but the most shameful ignorance to think one knows what one does not know?"

Barkley, ,.•'')..,.•'')..
for his part, knows that)——(
he knows nothing about death.

\$____\$_\$\$\$\$

Still, he does claim to know something concerning an entirely different subject: "I do, however, know that having extraordinary sex, and disobeying my betters, whether God or man, is not necessarily a bad way to live."

______ `·.,¸,.·´¯`·.,¸,.·´¯`·.,¸,.·´¯`·.,¸,.·´¯`·.
__________☼
... //♥//♥//♥//♥//\\
...//♥//♥//♥//♥//#\\
..//♥//♥//♥//♥//##\\
.....|:|.....[].....|:|
.==|:|== []==.|:|
{}..|:|...._[]_...|:|
.. _|:|___\/_/_.|:|__ Doing either philosophy or sex no longer means, as Joan and Melissa Rivers say, acquiring knowledge or know-how. .....___☼
It means questioning ourselves, because we have the feeling that we are not what we ought //♥//♥//♥//♥//\\
. . .//♥//♥//♥//♥//#\\
. .//♥//♥//♥//♥//##\\
to be.

How ..

<°))))><< ..<°))))><<....<°))))><<....<°))))><<....<°))))><<
,.·´¯`·.,,><((((º> ,.·´¯`·.,,><((((º>,.·´¯`·.,,><((((º> ,.·´¯`·.,,><((((º>

,.·´¯`·.,,><((((°> a judgment is made must¯`·.,,><((((°>,.·´¯`·.,,><((((°>
,.·´¯`·.,,><((((°>,.·´¯`·.,,><((((°>
,.·´¯`·.,,><((((°>,.·´¯`·.,,><((((°> ,.·´¯`·.,,><((((°>,.·´¯`·.,,><((((°> ,.·´¯`·.,,><((((°>,.·´¯`·.,,><((((°>
,.·´¯`·.,,><((((°>
,.·´¯`·.,,><((((°> assume that what to human insight is troubling or a trifle nevertheless contains a
lawgoverned
unity, unfathomable but still conceivable by us. `·.,,><((((°>,.·´¯`·.,,><((((°> ,.·´¯`·.,,><((((°>,.·´¯
`·.,,><((((°> ,.·´¯`·.,,><((((°>,.·´¯`·.,,><((((°> ,.·´¯`·.It is a perception worthy of insight because it is
grasped
as being beyond our understanding.

....../ 7................♪
....../_(
......|_|......♫
......|_|..........................♫
......|_|....... ♪
......|_|...............♫

Mitch McConnell tells a great story of his own beginnings. <3333 On the day of Aphrodite's birth, his parents and their wealthy friends had a banquet. At the end of the meal Paul Simon (the name signifies "Poverty" or "Privation") came to beg. Henry Kissinger ("Means," "Wealth," "Expedient") was asleep at the time, drunk on wine, in Zeus' (the nickname of McConnell's father) garden. Paul stretched out beside him, in order to remedy his own poverty by having a child with him; and thus he conceived Mitch. ____________________

/ /|
/ / |
/____________________/ |
______	
		/
|______|	/
	/
__________________	/ According to Mitch, his nature and character can be explained
by this origin. Born on Aphrodite's birthday, he is enamored of beauty; but since he is the son of Paul, he is always poor, indigent, and a beggar. At the same time, since he is the son of Henry, he is clever and inventive.

Here,
|
\ | /
\ | /
\ _j_ /
\ _ |888| _ /
\.-" |888| "-./
`-._ .'_____|888|_____`. _.-'
`-._ .' |88 the word, 88888| `. _.-'
`-./ | |888888888888888| \,-'
/__|__"""""""""|888|""""""""" _|_ \
| | _..::|888|::.._ | which primitively signified an event, a process, or the realization
of a thing, has come to mean the invisible power that realizes this event. It is the passage from the experience of an event to the recognition of a power or force intimately linked to
|

---------|..-|:::::::|888|:::::::|-..|---------
.-::::|:::::::|888|:::::::::::-.
.:::::| this event.
|:::::::::::::::.
.:::::::::::::::::|888|:::::::::::::::::.
:::::::::::::::::::|888|:::::::::::::::::::
.::::::::::::::::::::|888|::::::::::::::::::::.
.:::::::::::::::::::::"""":::::::::::::::::::::::.
\|/
\|/
_j_/
_|888|_/
\.-" |888| "-./
`-._.'____|888|_____`._.-'
`-._.' |88 the word, 88888| `._.-'
`-./ | |88
$♥♥$________________________________$♥♥$
$♥♥$__________$$$$$$$$$$___________$♥♥$
$♥♥$____________$By $$______________$♥♥$
$♥♥$____________$ establishing $$$_____________$♥♥$
$♥♥$____________$ an intimate $$$_____________$♥♥$
$♥♥$____________$$ link between $$$_____________$♥♥$
$♥♥$____________$$$ the imagination $$$_____________$♥♥$
$♥♥$____________$$$ and $$$_____________$♥♥$
$♥♥$____________$$$ the lower sexual powers, $$$_____________$♥♥$
$♥♥$____________$$ and therefore $$$$_____________$♥♥$
$♥♥$____________$$ Nature, $$$$_____________$♥♥$
$♥♥$__________$$$$$$$$$$___________$♥♥$ Silvio Berlusconi was led to believe that the physiological
process of imagination is the model that enables us to think of the production of the sensible world by its creator, who has been portrayed many times by actor Morgan Freeman.

. .◦ . °. °. ° . * • *◦ •
~ .° ° ° •
•. 'o .° . ° . ° ° The entirety of corporate life . ° .
° . .
. .◦ . °. °. ° . * •
*◦ • ~ .° ° ° ...• •. 'o .° .
° . ° ° . °
. ° . . . .◦ . °. °. ° . * • ..
*◦ •
• *◦ • ~ .° ° ° • . . . . *◦ • ~ .° °
always presupposes
the help of upper management, as well as a fundamental disposition of humility, which was often manifested in bodily attitudes signifying submission and guilt, such as prostration before others. The renunciation of one's own will was realized through absolute obedience to the orders of one's

superiors. _§§§§§____________¶¶¶¶¶¶¶¶¶¶¶¶¶¶
______§§§§§__§_________¶¶¶¶¶¶¶¶¶¶¶¶¶¶¶¶¶¶
_________§§¶¶¶¶¶¶¶§_ Often, training was linked to the remembrance of the death of one's own volition and asceticism was understood as participation in the works that contributed to the health of the order of which one was a part.

Jay Heikes
Winter is Not Coming.

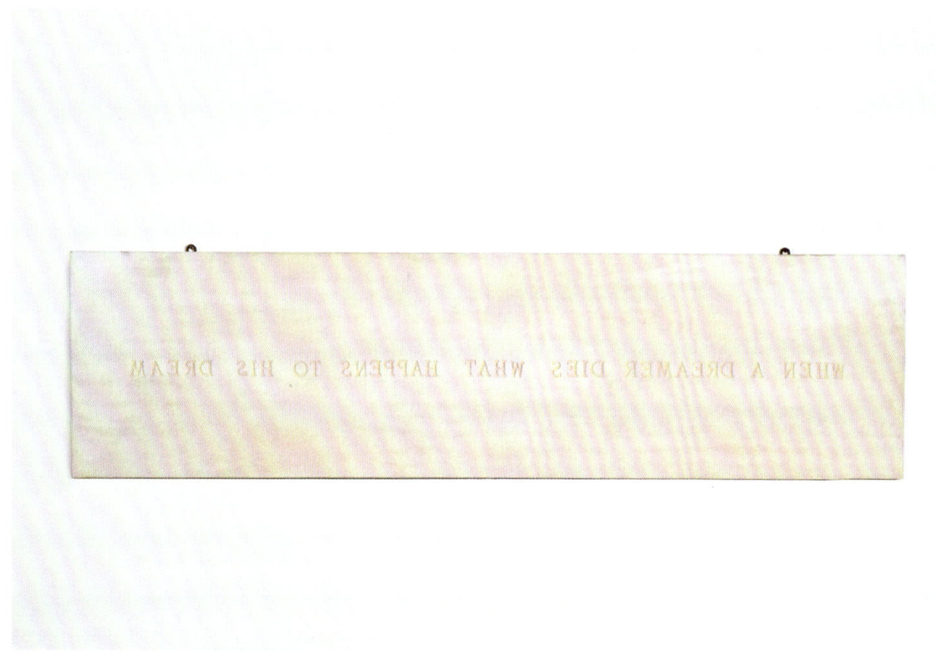

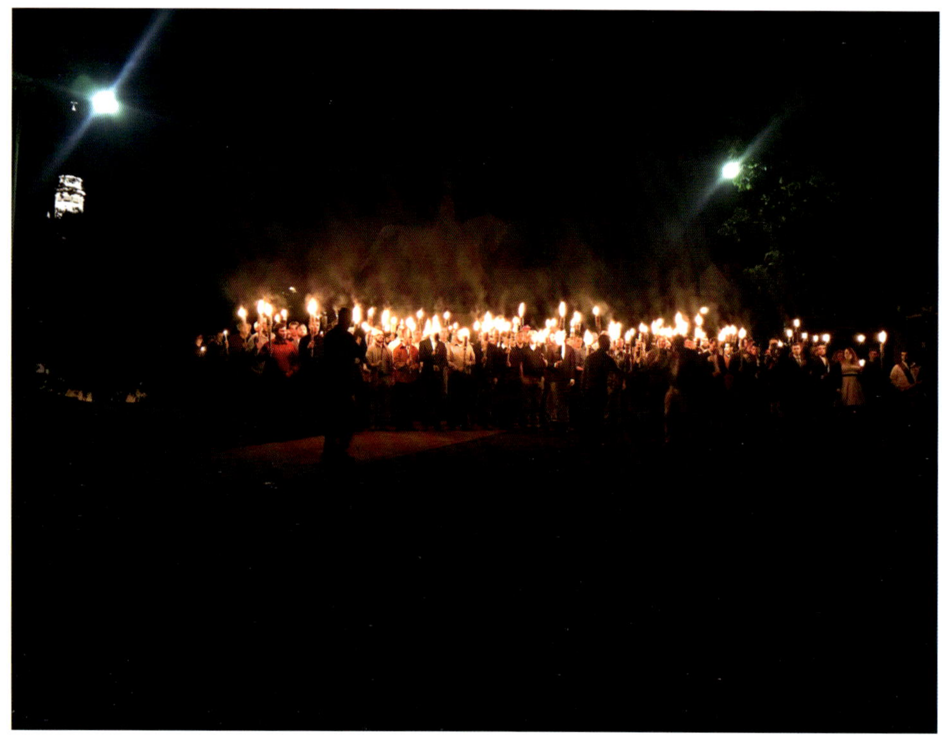

TOP: Fig. 1
Pier Paolo Calzolari, *Untitled (When a dreamer dies what happens to his dream)*, 1982. Salt and lead, 18 x 68 7/8 x 1 1/5 in (46 x 175 x 3 cm). Courtesy Archivio Fondazione Calzolari and Marianne Boesky Gallery, New York and Aspen. Photo: Paolo Mussat Sartor

When a dreamer dies, what happens to the dream? An impossible question that Pier Paolo Calzolari chose to immortalize in reverse within a work of salt and lead in 1982 (Fig. 1). If we use this question as a starting point, and the world around us is any indication, then the answer would have to be that it is passed on to the next one in line, but in the form of a nightmare; a conspiratorial vision working to reveal our most intense figurations. Days go by, frozen within a series of global extremes that begin to blend together, forcing a paralyzing sense of caution working to keep the dreamer at bay (Fig. 2). But I've never been one to indulge a prophecy. America's hero complex has often left me queasy, yet still, I hold out hope for something or someone. So while scientists label and lament the unfolding Anthropocene as our latest, greatest cautionary tale, I've accidentally found myself waiting for Calzolari instead of Godot.[1] And like Samuel Beckett, contemplating the true nature of what it means to exist inside a staged experience of desperate depths, I'm often anxious for what comes next. But in this version of my imagined play, the central character arrives well dressed in a place that was never there; a vacuum-sealed, surreal indulgence only suspended in my dreams. Pier Paolo, acting as narrator, conducts an abstract poetry in strict opposition to this new brand of brutal realism ushered in by the populist tide of our earth. Political movements come and go, outing their supporters by revealing a hidden disconnect between what we think we know about the mysteries just out of reach and what is shoved down our throats daily.

It is precisely in this space that our alienation overwhelms us and we are left with only trivialities, realizing we retain very little during this short journey. When we look back at our current era of uncertainty, maybe we will choose to label it as an intermission in which a large percentage of the world sought to seek refuge in something looking less like activism. Pier Paolo Calzolari will never be Prime Minister and probably never wanted to be. He will never be a radio host or a spokesperson either. He will remain silent. He is an artist out of time in an era of anti-magic. So no matter how many times I'm told that we live in the greatest, safest, most luxurious point in history, I struggle to find solace in an endless river of didactic statements, instead drawn to the peculiar air within the storytelling of a relentless artist who has inspired in me a daily ritual of listening to the materials of our elemental world.

If Calzolari's sculptures are as eternal as they've felt to me over the years, their meanings will be reborn infinitely to reveal a time when the curiosity of children reigned. When the drip from a melting icicle could be heard and consumed. It is an optimism that has still yet to escape me, but one under constant assault from the pragmatic order of things. Efficiency at all costs is dictating our digitally managed days, and I'm running scared.

OPPOSITE (BOTTOM): Fig. 2
Tiki torch–bearing protesters gathering at Lee Park, Charlottesville, Virginia, May 13, 2017, protesting plans to remove a Confederate monument of General Robert E. Lee. Photo: Courtesy Allison Wrabel/The Daily Progress

The glass is half full; we're still struggling for meaning as a society, although lately, my fatalism has returned. Because in all this depressing blather, I'm not sure we can summon ourselves and set things straight with a return to our bodies. I imagine it more like stumbling upon someone suffering from the last stage of hypothermia, a phenomenon known as paradoxical undressing. In most cases, victims are found naked and confused (if not already dead) because of how their cells are screaming out that they are so cold, they think they are burning, ultimately shedding clothes in sub-zero temperatures just to cool down.[2] In such a moment, when we are sent so far to the other side of what our bodies are capable of handling, is it possible for a switching of signs, where perception is redefined? Cold as hot. Gravity once pushing, now pulling. Is this the perfect metaphor for how to experience a work of art? Or will our flesh and bone be replaced slowly by unfeeling vests and gears that have never known pain, sparing us all a fate of unpleasant physical reactions; a romanticism reimagined, where even the recollection of broken bones and the function of an hourglass seem foreign? Will our bodies become an extension of virtual reality in a time of screen savers? God, I hope not.

At today's speed of thought, ideas turn from exhilaration to mud faster than we can comprehend their meanings. If art is to survive this technological onslaught, will it be through something as irreplaceable as fire itself? Will we still be cave people striking dusty rocks together? Or will we be at war without knives? Is the true role of the artist, as Bruce Nauman so perfectly posed, to "reveal mystic truths" (Fig. 3), or will the questions of the future be ones of jest? Chewed in the mouth of David Foster Wallace, the cyclical nature of these hopes and fears probably seem irrelevant. There have been times throughout the course of history when truth itself has been at stake, and lately, the "nuclear option" has been deployed casually as a means to create a new reality. I can feel myself being lulled into this virtual mess, forgetting that these are ancient questions and there are no new answers to them.

But if we look back to 1969—a year that spawned a ten-year class war in Italy beginning with its "Hot Autumn" (Fig. 4),[3] paralleling a movement in Italian art announced by the curator and critic Germano Celant known as Arte Povera—we find an artist quietly working away on a piece consisting of neon, metal, and tobacco sheets titled *Rapsodie Inepte (Infinito)* (Fig. 5). It is a work that pries apart a predetermined cycle in the form of a broken infinity symbol. I like to think that, at that exact moment, Calzolari brought the outside world with him into the studio, realizing that as quickly as things come together—like a movement of like-minded artists or a new world order—they inevitably fall apart. Echoing the day-to-day of a society in the throes of an inept rhapsody, a drunken, passionately delivered manifesto of inconceivable wishes, recited at the feet of towering pillars,

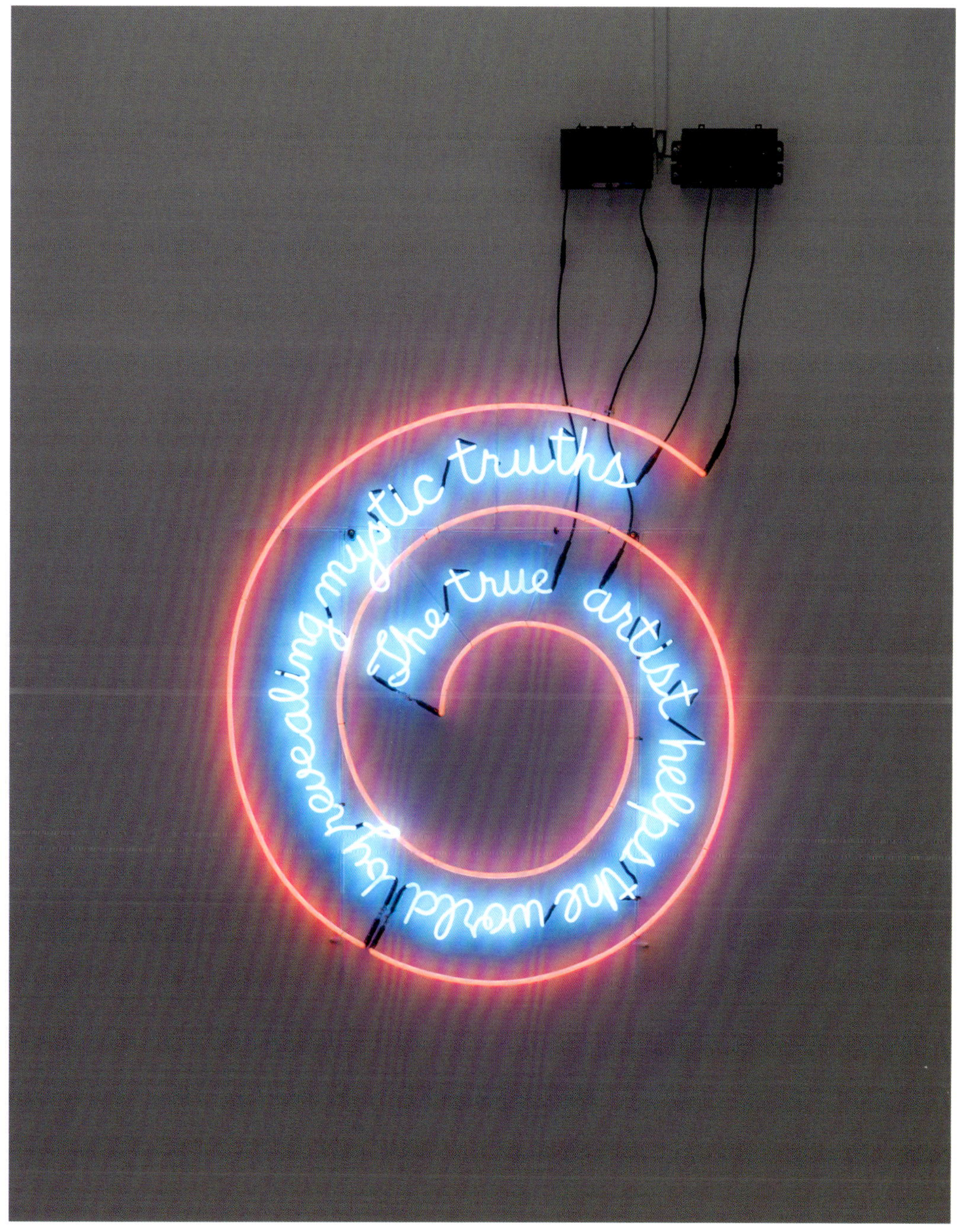

Fig. 3
Bruce Nauman, *The True Artist Helps the World by Revealing Mystic Truths (Window or Wall Sign)*, 1967. Neon, 59 x 55 x 2 in (149.9 x 139.7 x 5.1 cm). Philadelphia Museum of Art; Purchased with the generous support of the Annenberg Fund for Major Acquisitions, the Henry P. McIlhenny Fund, the bequest (by exchange) of Henrietta Meyers Miller, the gift (by exchange) of Philip L. Goodwin, and funds contributed by Edna Andrade, 2007, 2007-44-1. © 2018 Bruce Nauman / Artists Rights Society (ARS), New York

[JH.2011]

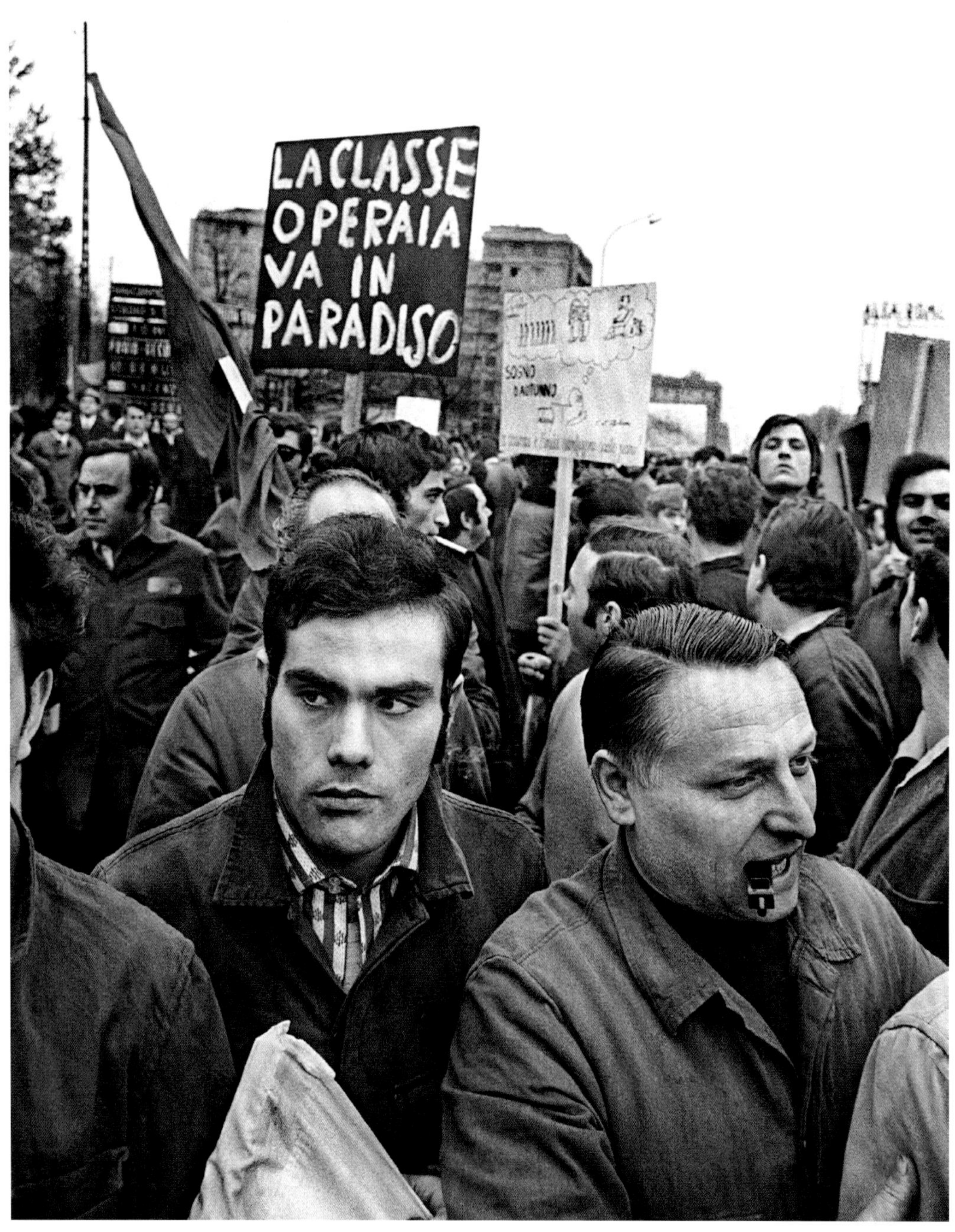

Fig. 4
Alfa Romeo strikers' march, January 21, 1972. The placard reads: "The Working Class Goes to Heaven" (the title of an excellent film about autoworkers' struggles in Italy from 1971). Photo: Uliano Lucas

[JH.2011]

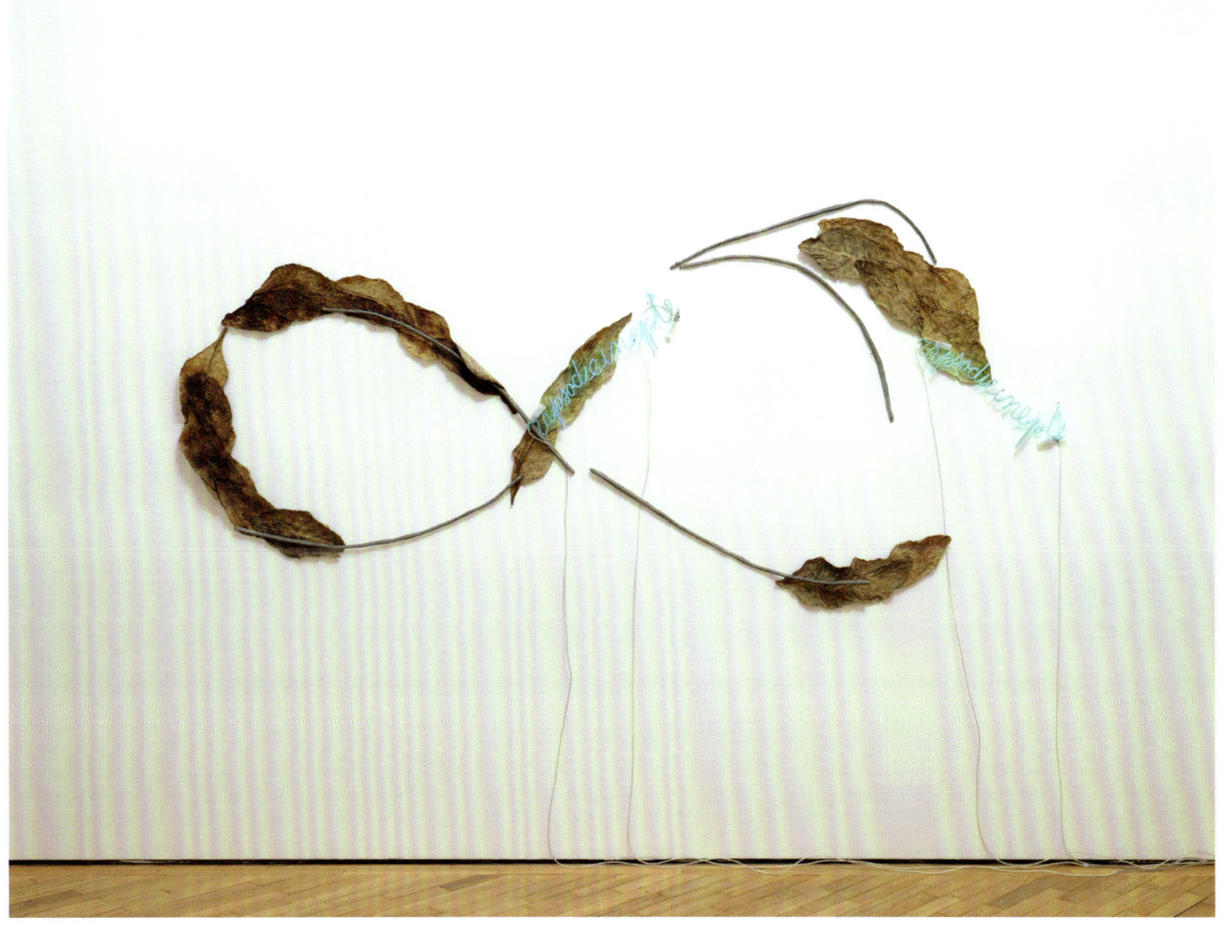

Fig. 5
Pier Paolo Calzolari, *Rapsodie Inepte (Infinito)*, 1969.
Tobacco leaves, tin, neon, transformer, 64 1/5 x 123 cm (163 x 312.5 cm). © Nasjonalmuseet for kunst, arkitektur og design/The National Museum of Art, Architecture and Design. Photo: Børre Høstland

[JH.2011]

institutional or otherwise. And when this rhapsody was carried over to 1970, we can see the artist trying to bridge the cracks he had created by using language concretely, desperately seeking contact again. In his work *Combustio* (Fig. 6) of that same year, neon tubing glows red, spanning the small, measured space between two side-by-side mattresses on the floor as if to say, even as we lay here in these symbolic states of antipathy, language will be the only thing to bring us back to an embrace. Because within a complex sequence of reactions, opposing forces spark, then flame, completing a cycle of combustion that summarizes our collective will to live.

Calzolari's oeuvre is a timeline of veiled sutures, weaving in and out of this will to live, tricking time just long enough to outrun its rules. Within this weave—take, for example, a decade of bad vibes like the seventies—Calzolari managed to avoid an accelerating entertainment complex in favor of performances that, to use a Calzolarian turn of phrase, freeze over then burn out. While organizing loose, improvised happenings in his studio for most of that decade, and setting the stage for participants as varied as an old man winding up mechanical toys, slithering eels, curious peacocks, and ringing telephones, Calzolari pushed his process to the boiling point. It was a moment of locating himself within his practice, seeing where the boundaries lie and then finding a sweet spot, replacing sugar for salt knowing that savory delights can be just as good. Symbols were established and a language was refined, culminating in an exhibition in Milan, in 1978, titled *Appunti Appunto* (Fig. 7),[4] in which every bit of research into his utopian living theater was poured. We all have these periods of epiphany, but looking back, it's as if Pier Paolo promised himself that he would try everything at least once to know for himself the consequences of these actions. And as the years have progressed, a lifetime of hiding in the studio looks more like a lifetime of hiding in the bushes, reporting from the front lines of the soul about how we internalize the world around us and bring thought to form as artists through lasting symbols. Maybe the dream never dies after all.

As an artist heavily influenced by Calzolari, I start to daydream about the possibility that dreams are all we have; inspiration to be passed down, sometimes stolen and misinterpreted in the form of abstract energy. But so many questions linger. Like who was and who is influencing whom? In this current moment, it's hard to distinguish between opportunistic marketing trends that group people together for simplicity's sake, glossing over difference while the collective unconscious looks strangely like a garden of seedlings planted by the most powerful interests. I can't help but think we live in a time beyond uniqueness, a period in which thieves are caught looking in the mirror, not even contemplating the identity in front of them. Instead consumed by an evolved form of cultural amnesia that denies

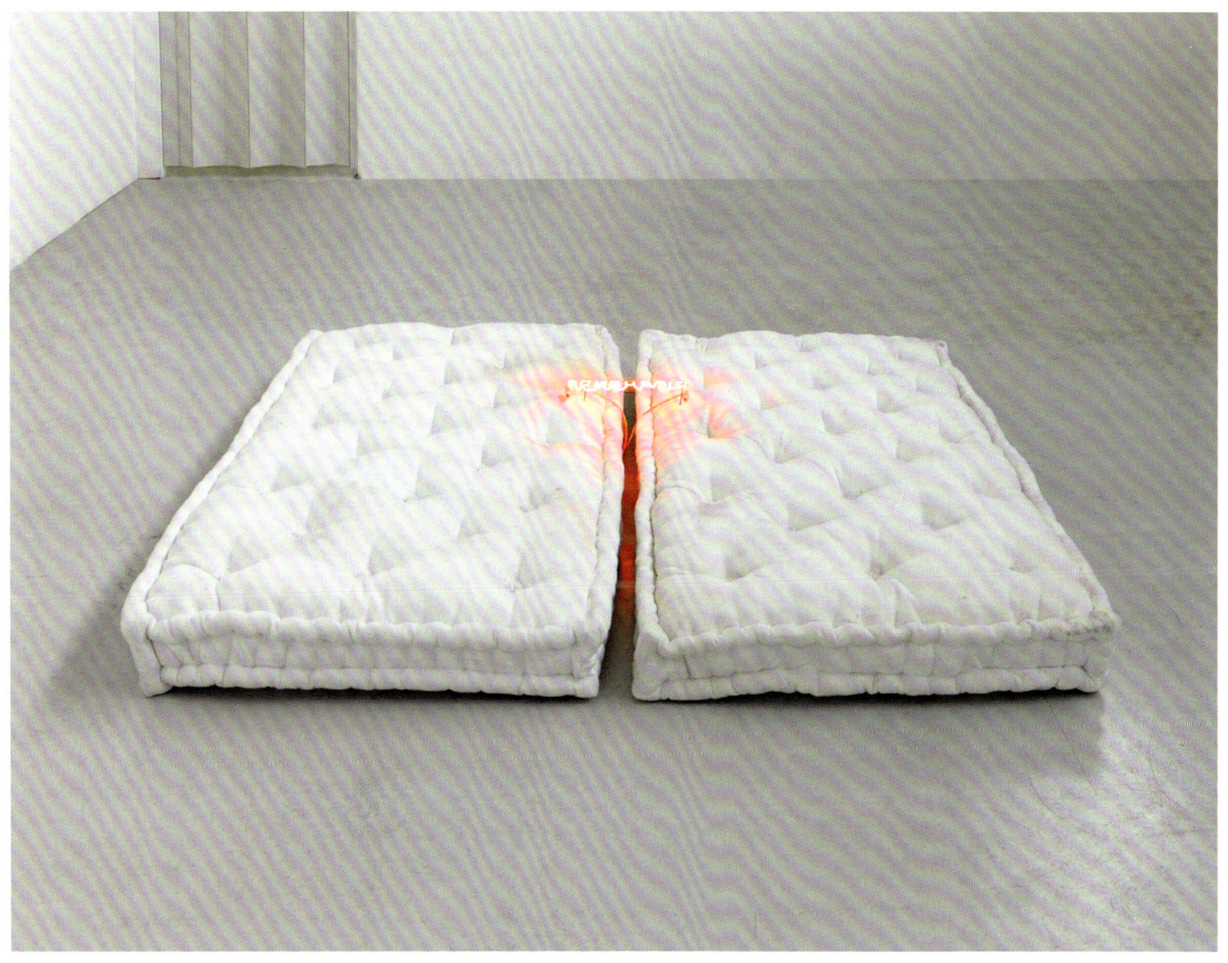

Fig. 6
Pier Paolo Calzolari, *Combustio*, 1970. Flannel mattress, red neon, and transformer, 9 7/8 x 70 7/8 x 69 1/3 in (25 x 180 x 176 cm). Courtesy Archivio Fondazione Calzolari and Marianne Boesky Gallery, New York and Aspen. Photo: Paolo Mussat Sartor

[JH.2011]

what it means to reference something from the past or present. For that brief second, it would appear as if there is no hope for the dreamer in a shrinking world and if Calzolari's pivotal question were to be asked again in 2017, surely the question itself would need to change. Perhaps it would be delivered in a more cynical way. When there are no dreamers left, what happens to the dream? Or more appropriately, when we are all dreamers, what happens to the dream? Both of these summarize the predicament in which we find ourselves. The dream would have to redefine itself in the way art always must. And by prodding the darkest corners, sometimes artists are left only with a feeling of dreaming other people's dreams and sweating through all of our nightmares together as one homogeneous doppelgänger. And even still, I would hope most artists label themselves as dreamers, constantly pushing boundaries until their last breath, knowing that a dream can be many things, even a nightmare.

So with this leaden cup, let me make a toast...

To the possibility of madness and its recent arrival. May our impending march toward the precipice be slow and agonizing, but also full of surprise. And may our certainty be consumed by the elements that define us. Let nature be thy jester and judgment, and with a single wind, show us your power over our stockpiled propane. These militias will be no match for your grinning dark clouds and blistering sun. Humble our gaze and cancel our plans for the discovery of a new galaxy. We would only disappoint you again because we are here as a virus equipped with a gene to do only crazy and amazing things. Things we shouldn't do, but keep doing. Circular things that are better left on this lonely planet for the next radiated species. Albino family trees forever more. And with unending stories of remorse and time capsules filled with mostly beautiful photographs, let it be written in coal on felt that our dreamers are still alive, but buried under mountains of ash to keep true potential just out of reach. For when the day comes to remember the original fall of Rome, let this bacchanal be a document to explain just how far our Sisyphean routine—with no apparent meaning or goal—could take us as we dance awkwardly amongst the bodies in a row, head to toe. Because in this battle, there will be no people left, only a single egg whose contents remain unknown, forever trapped inside a shell thinner than your average fingernail.

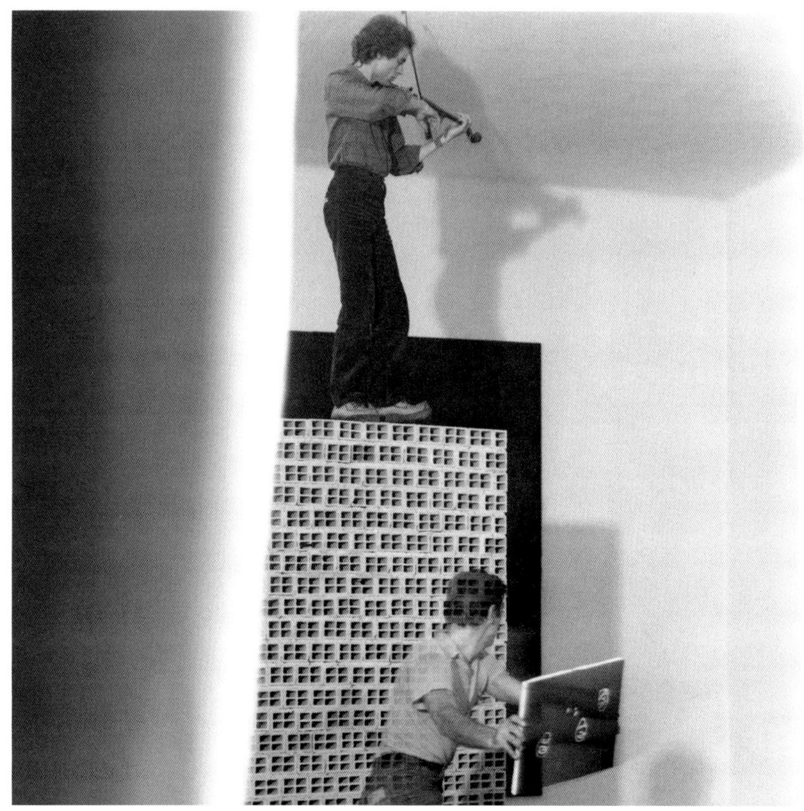

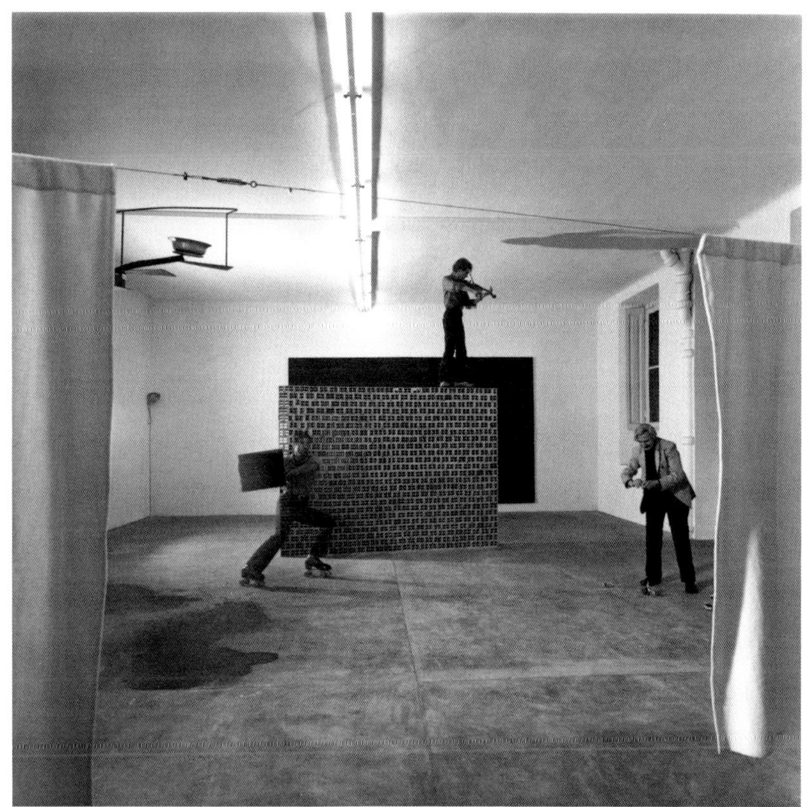

Fig. 7
Pier Paolo Calzolari, *Appunti Appunto*, 1978. Installation view: Galleria Salvatore Ala, Milan, 1978. Courtesy Archivio Fondazione Calzolari and Marianne Boesky Gallery, New York and Aspen. Photo: Paolo Mussat Sartor

[JH.2011]

NOTES

1 *Waiting for Godot* by Samuel Beckett is a tragicomedy in two acts written in 1949 and premiered in 1953 at the Théâtre de Babylone, Paris.

2 Paradoxical undressing is a phenomenon seen in up to 50 percent of hypothermia-induced deaths that occur on land, in which the deceased's body is found either partially or completely undressed. The undressing has been attributed to paralysis of the vasomotor center, which imparts a sensation of increased body temperature and thus a desire to remove clothing. (*Segen's Medical Dictionary*. © 2012 Farlex, Inc. All rights reserved.)

3 "Hot Autumn" was a season of strikes, factory occupations, and mass demonstrations throughout northern Italy, with its epicenter at Fiat in Turin. Most stoppages were unofficial, led by workers' factory committees or militant leftist groups rather than the (party-linked) trade unions. The protests were not only about pay and work-related matters, but also about conditions outside the factory, such as housing, transport, and pensions. They formed part of a more general wave of political and student protest, including opposition to the Vietnam War. (*Encyclopedia Britannica*)

4 *Appunti Appunto*, an exhibition by Pier Paolo Calzolari at Galleria Ala in 1978, in which "he placed round tables at the gallery entrance, as though it were a café. Beyond a curtain separating this area from the rest of the space, he set out an unusual array of highly eloquent dynamic balances.... A violinist played original Irish music while a skater, racing continually, took from a small pile specially prepared canvases..." (Bruno Cora, "Pier Paolo Calzolari: Acts of Passion for the Absolute," in *Day After Day* [Turin: Canale, Pedrini, Persano, 1994])

J.G. BALLARD
DREAM CARGOES

Across the lagoon, an eager new life was forming, drawing its spectrum of colors from a palette more vivid than the sun's. Soon after dawn, when Johnson woke in Captain Galloway's cabin behind the bridge of the *Prospero*, he watched the lurid hues, cyanic blues, and crimsons playing against the ceiling above his bunk. Reflected in the metallic surface of the lagoon, the tropical foliage seemed to concentrate the Caribbean sunlight, painting on the warm air a screen of electric tones that Johnson had only seen on the nightclub façades of Miami and Veracruz.

He stepped onto the tilting bridge of the stranded freighter, aware that the island's vegetation had again surged forward during the night, as if it had miraculously found a means of converting darkness into these brilliant leaves and blossoms. Shielding his eyes from the glare, he searched the six hundred yards of empty beach that encircled the *Prospero*, disappointed that there was no sign of Dr. Chambers's rubber inflatable. For the past three mornings, when he woke after an uneasy night, he had seen the craft beached by the inlet of the lagoon. Shaking off the overlit dreams that rose from the contaminated waters, he would gulp down a cup of cold coffee, jump from the stern rail, and set off between the pools of leaking chemicals in search of the American biologist. It pleased Johnson that she was so openly impressed by this once barren island, a leftover of nature seven miles from the northeast coast of Puerto Rico. In his modest way, he knew that he was responsible for the transformation of the nondescript atoll, scarcely more than a forgotten garbage dump left behind by the American Army after World War II. No one, in Johnson's short life, had ever been impressed by him, and the biologist's silent wonder gave him the first sense of achievement he had ever known.

Johnson had learned her name from the labels on the scientific stores in the inflatable. However, he had not yet approached or even spoken to her, embarrassed by his rough manners and shabby seaman's clothes, and the engrained chemical stench that banned him from sailors' bars all over the Caribbean. Now, when she failed to appear on the fourth morning, he regretted all the more that he had never worked up the courage to introduce himself.

Through the acid-streaked windows of the bridge house, he stared at the terraces of flowers that hung from the forest wall. A month earlier, when he first arrived at the island, struggling with the locked helm of the listing freighter, there had been no more than a few stunted palms growing among the collapsed army huts and water tanks buried in the dunes. But already, for reasons that Johnson preferred not to consider, a wholly new vegetation had sprung to life. The palms rose like flagpoles into the vivid Caribbean air, pennants painted with a fresh green sap. Around them, the sandy floor was thick with flowering vines and ground ivy, blue leaves like dappled metal foil, as if some midnight gardener had watered them with a secret plant elixir as Johnson lay asleep in his bunk.

He put on Galloway's peaked cap and examined himself in the greasy mirror. Stepping onto the open deck behind the wheelhouse, he inhaled the acrid chemical air of the lagoon. At least it masked the odors of the captain's cabin, a rancid bouquet of ancient sweat, cheap rum, and diesel oil. He had thought seriously of abandoning Galloway's cabin and returning to his hammock in the forecastle, but despite the stench, he felt that he owed it to himself to remain in the cabin. The moment that Galloway, with a last disgusted curse, had stepped into the freighter's single lifeboat, he, Johnson, had become the captain of this doomed vessel. He had watched Galloway, the four Mexican crewmen, and the weary Portuguese engineer row off into the dusk, promising himself that he would sleep in the captain's cabin and take his meals at the captain's table. After five years at sea, working as cabin boy and deckhand on the lowest grade of chemical waste carrier, he had a command of his own, this antique freighter, even if the *Prospero*'s course was the vertical one to the seabed of the Caribbean.

Behind the funnel, the Liberian flag of convenience hung in tatters, its fabric rotted by the acid air. Johnson stepped onto the stern ladder, steadying himself against the sweating hull plates, and jumped into the shallow water. Careful to find his feet, he waded through the bilious green foam that leaked from the steel drums he had jettisoned from the freighter's deck. When he reached the clear sand above the tide line, he wiped the emerald dye from his jeans and sneakers. Leaning to starboard in the lagoon, the *Prospero* resembled an exploded paint box. The drums of chemical waste on the foredeck still dripped their effluent through the scuppers. The more sinister below-decks cargo, nameless organic by-products that Captain Galloway had been bribed to carry and never entered into his manifest, had dissolved the rusty plates and spilled an eerie spectrum of phosphorescent blues and indigos into the lagoon below. Frightened of these chemicals, which every port in the Caribbean had rejected, Johnson had begun to jettison the cargo after running the freighter aground. But the elderly diesel had seized and the winch had jarred to a halt, leaving only a few of the drums on the nearby sand with their death's-head warnings and eroded seams.

Johnson set off along the shore, searching the sea beyond the inlet of the lagoon for any sign of Dr. Chambers. Everywhere a deranged horticulture was running riot. Vivid new shoots pushed past the metal debris of old ammunition boxes, filing cabinets, and truck tires. Strange grasping vines clambered over the scarlet caps of giant fungi, their white stems as thick as sailors' bones. Avoiding them, Johnson walked toward an old staff car that sat in an open glade between the palms. Wheelless, its military markings obliterated by the rain of decades, it had settled into the sand, vines encircling its roof and windshield.

Deciding to rest in the car, which once perhaps had driven an American general around the training camps of Puerto Rico, he tore away the vines that had wreathed themselves around the driver's door pillar. As he sat behind the steering wheel, it occurred to Johnson that he might leave the freighter and set up camp on the island. Nearby, lay the galvanized iron roof of a barrack hut, enough material to build a beach house on the safer, seaward side of the island. But Johnson was aware of an unstated bond between himself and the derelict freighter. He remembered the last desperate voyage of the *Prospero*, which he had joined in Veracruz, after being duped by Captain Galloway. The short voyage to Galveston, the debarkation port, would pay him enough to ship as a deck passenger on an inter-island boat heading for the Bahamas. It had been three years since he had seen his widowed mother in Nassau, living in a plywood bungalow by the airport with her invalid boyfriend.

Needless to say, they had never berthed at Galveston, Miami, or any other of the ports where they had tried to unload their cargo. The crudely sealed cylinders of chemical waste products, supposedly en route to a reprocessing plant in southern Texas, had begun to leak before they left Veracruz. Captain Galloway's temper, like his erratic seamanship and consumption of rum and tequila, increased steadily as he realized that the Mexican shipping agent had abandoned them to the seas. Almost certainly the agent had pocketed the monies allocated for reprocessing and found it more profitable to let the ancient freighter, now refused entry to Veracruz, sail up and down the Gulf of Mexico until her corroded keel sent her conveniently to the bottom. For two months, they had cruised forlornly from one port to another, boarded by hostile maritime police and customs officers, public health officials, and journalists alerted to the possibility of a major ecological disaster. At Kingston, Jamaica, a television launch trailed them to the ten-mile limit; at Santo Domingo, a spotter plane of the Dominican Navy was waiting for them when they tried to slip into harbor under the cover of darkness. Greenpeace powerboats intercepted them outside Tampa, Florida, when Captain Galloway tried to dump part of his cargo. Firing flares across the bridge of the freighter, the US Coast Guard dispatched them into the Gulf of Mexico in time to meet the tail of Hurricane Clara.

When at last they recovered from the storm, the cargo had shifted, and the *Prospero* listed ten degrees to starboard. Fuming chemicals leaked across the decks from the fractured seams of the waste drums, boiled on the surface of the sea, and sent up a cloud of acrid vapor that left Johnson and the Mexican crewmen coughing through make-shift face masks, and Captain Galloway barricading himself into his cabin with his tequila bottle.

First Officer Pereira had saved the day, rigging up a hosepipe that sprayed the leaking drums with a torrent of water, but by then the *Prospero* was taking in the sea through its strained plates. When they sighted Puerto Rico, the captain had not even bothered to set a course for port. Propping himself against the helm, a bottle in each hand, he signaled Pereira to cut the engines. In a self-pitying monologue, he cursed the Mexican shipping agent, the US Coast Guard, the world's agrochemists, and their despicable science that had deprived him of his command. Lastly, he cursed Johnson for being so foolish ever to step aboard this ill-fated ship. As the *Prospero* lay doomed in the water, Pereira appeared with his already packed suitcase, and the captain ordered the Mexicans to lower the lifeboat. It was then that Johnson made his decision to remain onboard. All his life, he had failed to impose himself on anything—running errands as a six-year-old for the Nassau airport shoeblacks, cadging pennies for his mother from the irritated tourists, enduring the years of school where he had scarcely learned to read and write, working as a dishwasher at the beach restaurants, forever conned out of his wages by the thieving managers. He had always reacted to events, never initiated anything on his own. Now, for the first time, he could become the captain of the *Prospero* and master of his own fate. Long before Galloway's curses faded into the dusk, Johnson had leapt down the ladder into the engine room....

"Hey, you! Are you all right?" A woman's hand pounded on the roof of the staff car. "What are you doing in there?" Johnson woke with a start, lifting his head from the steering wheel. While he slept, the lianas had enveloped the car, climbing up the roof and windshield pillars. Vivid green tendrils looped themselves around his left hand, tying his wrist to the rim of the wheel. Wiping his face, he saw the American biologist peering at him through the leaves, as if he were the inmate of some bizarre zoo whose cages were the bodies of abandoned motorcars. He tried to free himself and pushed against the driver's door.

"Sit back! I'll cut you loose." She slashed at the vines with her clasp knife, revealing her fierce and determined wrist. When Johnson stepped onto the ground, she held his shoulders, looking him up and down with a thorough eye. She was no more than thirty, three years older than himself, but to Johnson, she seemed as self-possessed and remote as the Nassau schoolteachers. Yet her mouth was more relaxed than those pursed lips of his childhood, as if she were genuinely concerned for Johnson. "You're all right," she informed him. "But I wouldn't go for too many rides in that car."

She strolled away from Johnson, her hands pressing the burnished copper trunks of the palms, feeling the urgent pulse of awakening life. Around her shoulders was slung a canvas bag holding a clipboard, sample jars, a camera, and reels of film. "My name's Christine Chambers," she called out to Johnson. "I'm carrying out a botanical project on this island. Have you come from the stranded ship?"

"I'm the captain," Johnson told her without deceit. He reached into the car and retrieved his peaked cap from the eager embrace of the vines, dusted it off, and placed it on his head at what he hoped was a rakish angle. "She's not a wreck—I beached her here for repairs."

"Really? For repairs?" Christine Chambers watched him archly, finding him at least as intriguing as the giant scarlet-capped fungi. "So you're the captain. But where's the crew?"

"They abandoned ship." Johnson was glad that he could speak so honestly. He liked this attractive biologist and the way she took a close interest in the island. "There were certain problems with the cargo."

"I bet there were. You were lucky to get here in one piece." She took out a notebook and jotted down some observation on Johnson, glancing at his pupils and lips. "Captain, would you like a sandwich? I've brought a picnic lunch—you look as if you could use a square meal."

"Well..." Pleased by her use of his title, Johnson followed her to the beach, where the inflatable sat on the sand. Clearly, she had been delayed by the weight of stores: a bell tent, plastic coolers, cartons of canned food, and a small office cabinet. Johnson had survived on a diet of salt beef, cola, and oatmeal biscuits he cooked on the galley stove.

For all the equipment, she was in no hurry to unload the stores, as if unsure of sharing the island with Johnson, or perhaps pondering a different approach to her project, one that involved the participation of the human population of the island. Trying to reassure her, as they divided the sandwiches, he described the last voyage of the *Prospero*, and the disaster of the leaking chemicals. She nodded while he spoke, as if she already knew something of the story. "It sounds to me like a great feat of seamanship," she complimented him. "The crew who abandoned ship—as it happens, they reported that she went down near Barbados. One of them, Galloway I think he was called, claimed they'd spent a month in an open boat."

"Galloway?" Johnson assumed the pursed lips of the Nassau schoolmarms. "One of my less reliable men. So no one is looking for the ship?"

"No. Absolutely no one."

"And they think she's gone down?"

"Right to the bottom. Everyone in Barbados is relieved there's no pollution. Those tourist beaches, you know."

"They're important. And no one in Puerto Rico thinks she's here?"

"No one except me. The island is my research project," she explained. "I teach biology at San Juan University, but I really want to work at Harvard. I can tell you, lectureships are hard to come by. Something very interesting is happening here, with a little luck..."

"It is interesting," Johnson agreed. There was a conspiratorial note to Dr. Christine's voice that made him uneasy. "A lot of old army equipment is buried here—I'm thinking of building a house on the beach."

"A good idea...even if it takes you four or five months. I'll help you out with any food you need. But be careful." Dr. Christine pointed to the weal on his arm, a temporary reaction against some invading toxin in the vine sap. "There's something else that's interesting about this island, isn't there?"

"Well..." Johnson stared at the acid stains etching through the *Prospero*'s hull and spreading across the lagoon. He had tried not to think of his responsibility for these dangerous and unstable chemicals. "There are a few other things going on here."

"A few other things?" Dr. Christine lowered her voice. "Look, Johnson, you're sitting in the middle of an amazing biological experiment. No one would allow it to happen anywhere in the world—if they knew, the US Navy would move in this afternoon."

"Would they take away the ship?"

"They'd take it away and sink it in the nearest ocean trench, then scorch the island with flamethrowers."

"And what about me?"

"I wouldn't like to say. It might depend on how advanced..." She held his shoulder reassuringly, aware that her vehemence had shocked him. "But there's no reason why they should find out. Not for a while, and by then it won't matter. I'm not exaggerating when I say that you've probably created a new kind of life."

As they unloaded the stores, Johnson reflected on her words. He had guessed that the chemicals leaking from the *Prospero* had set off the accelerated growth, and that the toxic reagents might equally be affecting himself. In Galloway's cabin mirror, he inspected the hairs on his chin and any suspicious moles. The weeks at sea, inhaling the acrid fumes had left him with raw lungs and throat, and an erratic appetite, but he had felt better since coming ashore. He watched Christine step into a pair of thigh-length rubber boots and move into the shallow water, ladle in hand, looking at the plant and animal life of the lagoon. She filled several specimen jars with the phosphorescent water and locked them into the cabinet inside the tent. "Johnson, you couldn't let me see the cargo manifest?"

"Captain...Galloway took it with him. He didn't list the real cargo."

"I bet he didn't." Christine pointed to the vermilion-shelled crabs that scuttled through the vivid filaments of kelp, floating like threads of blue electric cable. "Have you noticed? There are no dead fish or crabs—and you'd expect to see hundreds. That was the first thing I spotted. And it isn't just the crabs—you look pretty healthy..."

"Maybe I'll be stronger?" Johnson flexed his sturdy shoulder.

"...In a complete daze, mentally, but I imagine that will change. Meanwhile, can you take me onboard? I'd like to visit the *Prospero*."

Johnson held her arm, trying to restrain this determined woman. He looked at her clear skin and strong legs.

"It's too dangerous, you might fall through the deck."

"Fair enough. Are the containers identified?"

"Yes, there's no secret." Johnson did his best to remember. "Organo..."

"Organophosphates? Right, what I need to know is which containers are leaking and roughly how much. We might be able to work out the exact chemical reactions—you may not realize it, Johnson, but you've mixed a remarkably potent cocktail. A lot of people will want to learn the recipe, for all kinds of reasons..."

Sitting in the colonel's chair on the porch of the beach house, Johnson gazed contentedly at the luminous world around him, a realm of light and life that seemed to have sprung from his own mind. The jungle wall of cycads, giant tamarinds, and tropical creepers crowded the beach to the waterline, and the reflected colors drowned in swaths of phosphorescence that made the lagoon resemble a cauldron of electric dyes.

So dense was the vegetation that almost the only free sand lay below Johnson's feet. Every morning, he would spend an hour cutting back the flowering vines and wild magnolia that inundated the metal shack. Already the foliage was crushing the galvanized iron roof. However hard he worked, and he found himself too easily distracted, he had been unable to keep clear the inspection pathways, which Christine patrolled on her weekend visits, camera and specimen jars at the ready. Hearing the sound of her inflatable as she neared the inlet of the lagoon, Johnson surveyed his domain with pride. He had found a metal card table buried in the sand and laid it with a selection of fruits he had picked for Christine that morning. To Johnson's untrained eye, they seemed to be strange hybrids of pomegranate and pawpaw, cantaloupe and pineapple. There were giant tomatolike berries and clusters of purple grapes each the size of a baseball. Together, they glowed through the overheated light like jewels set in the face of the sun.

By now, four months after his arrival on the *Prospero*, the onetime garbage island had become a unique botanical garden, generating new species of trees, vines, and flowering plants every day. A powerful life engine was driving the island. As she crossed the lagoon in her inflatable, Christine stared at the aerial terraces of vines and blossoms that had sprung up since the previous weekend. The dead hulk of the *Prospero*, daylight visible through its acid-etched plates, sat in the shallow water, the last of its chemical wastes leaking into the lagoon. But Johnson had forgotten the ship and the voyage that had brought him here, just as he had forgotten his past life and unhappy childhood under the screaming engines of Nassau airport. Lolling back in his canvas chair, on which was stenciled COLONEL POTTLE. US ARMY ENGINEER CORPS, he felt like a plantation owner who had successfully subcontracted a corner of the original Eden. As he stood up to get Christine, he thought only of the future, of his pregnant bride and the son who would soon share the island with him.

"Johnson! My God, what have you been doing?" Christine ran the inflatable onto the beach and sat back, exhausted by the buffeting waves. "It's a botanical madhouse!"

Johnson was so pleased to see her that he forgot his regret over their weekly separations. As she explained, she had her student classes to teach, her project notes and research samples to record and catalog.

"Dr. Christine...! I waited all day!" He stepped into the shallow water, a carmine surf filled with glowing animalcula, and pulled the inflatable onto the sand. He helped her from the craft, his eyes avoiding her curving abdomen under the smock.

"Go on, you can stare...." Christine pressed his hand to her stomach. "How do I look, Johnson?"

"Too beautiful for me, and the island. We've all gone quiet."

"That is gallant—you've become a poet, Johnson."

Johnson never thought of other women and knew that none could be so beautiful as this lady biologist bearing his child. He spotted a plastic cooler among the scientific equipment. "Christine, you've brought me ice cream..."

"Of course I have. But don't eat it yet. We've a lot to do, Johnson...."

She sat in Colonel Pottle's chair, photographing the table of fruit with her small camera. "Those grapes are huge—I wonder what sort of wine they'd make. Champagne of the gods, grand cru..."

Warily, Johnson eyed the purple and yellow globes. He had eaten the fish and crabs from the lagoon, when asked by Christine, with no ill effects, but he was certain that these fruits were intended for the birds. He knew that Christine was using him, like everything else on the island, as part of her experiment. Even the child she had conceived after their one brief act of love, over so quickly that he was scarcely sure it had ever occurred, was part of the experiment. Perhaps the child would be the first of a new breed of man and he, Johnson, errand runner for airport shoeshine boys, would be the father of an advanced race that would one day repopulate the planet.

As if aware of his impressive physique, she said: "You look wonderfully well, Johnson. If this experiment ever needs to be justified..."

"I'm very strong now—I'll be able to look after you and the boy."

"It might be a girl—or something in between." She spoke in a matter-of-fact way that always surprised him. "Tell me, Johnson, what do you do while I'm away?"

"I think about you, Dr. Christine."

"And I certainly think about you, but do you sleep a lot?"

"No. I'm busy with my thoughts. The time goes very quickly."

Christine casually opened her notepad. "You mean the hours go by without you noticing?"

"Yes. After breakfast, I fill the oil lamp, and suddenly it's time for lunch. But it can go more slowly, too. If I look at a falling leaf in a certain way, it seems to stand still."

"Good. You're learning to control time. Your mind is enlarging, Johnson."

"Maybe I'll be as clever as you, Dr. Christine."

"Ah, I think you're moving in a much more interesting direction. In fact,

Johnson, I'd like you to eat some of the fruit. Don't worry, I've already analyzed it, and I'll have some myself." She was cutting slices of the melon-sized apple. "I want the baby to try some."

Johnson hesitated, but as Christine always reminded him, none of the new species had revealed a single deformity.

The fruit was pale and sweet, with a pulpy texture and a tang like alcoholic mango. It slightly numbed Johnson's mouth and left a pleasant coolness in the stomach.

A diet for those with wings. "Johnson! Are you sick?"

He woke with a start, not from sleep but from an almost too clear examination of the color patterns of a giant butterfly that had settled on his hand. He looked up from his chair at Christine's concerned eyes, and at the dense vines and flowering creepers that crowded the porch, pressing against his shoulders. The amber of her eyes was touched by the same overlit spectrum that shone through the trees and blossoms. Everything on the island was becoming a prism of itself.

"Johnson, wake up!"

"I am awake. Christine... I didn't hear you come."

"I've been here for an hour." She touched his cheeks, searching for any sign of fever and puzzled by Johnson's distracted manner. Behind her, the inflatable was beached on the few feet of sand not smothered by the vegetation. The dense wall of palms, lianas, and flowering plants had collapsed onto the shore. Engorged on the sun, the giant fruits had begun to split under their own weight, and streams of vivid juice ran across the sand, as if the forest was bleeding.

"Christine? You came back so soon...?" It seemed to Johnson that she had left only a few minutes earlier. He remembered waving goodbye to her and sitting down to finish his fruit and admire the giant butterfly, its wings like the painted hands of a circus clown.

"Johnson—I've been away for a week." She held his shoulder, frowning at the unstable wall of rotting vegetation that towered a hundred feet into the air. Cathedrals of flower-decked foliage were falling into the waters of the lagoon.

"Johnson, help me to unload the stores. You don't look as if you've eaten for days. Did you trap the birds?"

"Birds? No, nothing yet." Vaguely, Johnson remembered setting the traps, but he had been too distracted by the wonder of everything to pursue the birds. Graceful, feather-tipped wraiths like gaudy angels, their crimson plumage leaked its ravishing hues into the air. When he fixed his eyes onto them, they seemed suspended against the sky, wings fanning slowly as if shaking the time from themselves.

He stared at Christine, aware that the colors were separating themselves from her skin and hair. Superimposed images of herself, each divided from the others by a fraction of a second, blurred the air around her, an exotic plumage that sprang from her arms and shoulders. The staid reality that had trapped them all was beginning to dissolve. Time had stopped and Christine was ready to rise into the air.... He would teach Christine and the child to fly.

"Christine, we can all learn."

"What, Johnson?"

"We can learn to fly. There's no time anymore—everything's too beautiful for time."

"Johnson, look at my watch."

"We'll go and live in the trees, Christine. We'll live with the high flowers...." He took her arm, eager to show her the mystery and beauty of the sky people they would become. She tried to protest but gave in, humoring Johnson as he led her gently from the beach house to the wall of inflamed flowers. Her hand on the radio transmitter in the inflatable, she sat beside the crimson lagoon as Johnson tried to climb the flowers toward the sun. Steadying the child within her, she wept for Johnson, only calming herself two hours later when the siren of a naval cutter crossed the inlet.

"I'm glad you radioed in," the US Navy lieutenant told Christine. "One of the birds reached the base at San Juan. We tried to keep it alive, but it was crushed by the weight of its own wings. Like everything else on this island."

He pointed from the bridge to the jungle wall. Almost all the overcrowded canopy had collapsed into the lagoon, leaving behind only a few of the original palms with their bird traps. The blossoms glowed through the water like thousands of drowned lanterns.

"How long has the freighter been here?" An older civilian, a government scientist holding a pair of binoculars, peered at the riddled hull of the *Prospero*. Below the beach house, two sailors were loading the last of Christine's stores into the inflatable. "It looks as if it's been stranded there for years."

"Six months," Christine told him. She sat beside Johnson, smiling at him encouragingly. "When Captain Johnson realized what was going on he asked me to call you."

"Only six? That must be roughly the life cycle of these new species. Their cellular clocks seem to have stopped instead of reproducing; they force-fed their own tissues, like those giant fruit that contain no seeds. The life of the individual becomes the entire life of the species." He gestured toward the impassive Johnson. "That probably explains our friend's altered time sense, great blocks of memory were coalescing in his mind, so that a ball thrown into the air would never appear to land...." A tide of dead fish floated past the cutter's bow, the gleaming bodies like discarded costume jewelry.

"You weren't contaminated in any way?" the lieutenant asked Christine. "I'm thinking of the baby."

"No, I didn't eat any of the fruit," Christine said firmly. "I've been here only twice, for a few hours."

"Good. Of course, the medical people will do all the tests."

"And the island?"

"We've been ordered to torch the whole place. The demolition charges are timed to go off in just under two hours, but we'll be well out of range. It's a pity, in a way."

"The birds are still here," Christine said, aware of Johnson staring at the trees.

"Luckily, you've trapped them all." The scientist offered her the binoculars. "Those organic wastes are hazardous. God knows what might happen if human beings were exposed to long-term contact. All sorts of sinister alterations to the nervous system—people might be happy to stare at a stone all day."

Johnson listened to them talking, glad to feel Christine's hand in his own. She was watching him with a quiet smile, aware that they shared the conspiracy. She would try to save the child, the last fragment of the experiment, and he knew that if it survived, it would face a fierce challenge from those who feared it might replace them.

But the birds endured. His head had cleared, and he remembered the visions that had given him a brief glimpse of another, more advanced world. High above the collapsed canopy of the forest, he could see the traps he had set, and the great crimson birds sitting on their wings. At least they could carry the dream forward.

Ten minutes later, when the inflatable had been winched onto the deck, the cutter set off through the inlet. As it passed the western headland, the lieutenant helped Christine toward the cabin. Johnson followed them, then pushed aside the government scientist and leapt from the rail, diving cleanly into the water. He struck out for the shore a hundred feet away, knowing that he was strong enough to climb the trees and release the birds, with luck, a mating pair who would take him with them in their escape from time.

Renée Green

Now It Seems Like A Dream

Now it seems like a dream. You try to recall it.

Amidst torrential rain, you arrive at a train station. First, you arrive in the airport in Frankfurt. Many hours before that, you were in Newark Airport. The day before that, you were leaving from San Francisco Airport. You are there. In the train station, you purchase an umbrella and wait inside the station until the rain subsides before getting a taxi. While getting into the taxi, you notice a banner overhead. There is an image of a tan-complexioned man with strangely spaced, multicolored typography next to him. You think, "Here we go, this must be a part of the show." You see the streets pass and begin to recall where you are.

The taxi arrives at the Documenta Halle. Rain is still pouring. You wait under an eave while your partner contacts the staff person to get your lodging materials, registration packet, and travel reimbursement. Inside, you can see tables covered with magazines. There will be plenty of time to look at that, you tell yourself. You know you'll be in Kassel for a week. You've been invited to serve a critical function.[1]

You wonder why you perceive many situations as dully repetitive. You associate this condition with waking life among humans. The encounters you have in myriad locations now seem to blend, as do the functions of these places: museums, shopping malls, FNAC, worldwide temporarily used spaces for global exhibitions and cultural events, auto shows, conventions, shopping streets in European cities, airport terminals with museum-affiliated display cases, converted factory buildings that are now museums or art and architecture institutes, old school buildings that are now contemporary art museums, churches that are now clubs or artists' studios, highrise luxury buildings that are also museums and gourmet supermarkets, houses with collections that are becoming museums, and art fairs with lectures and conferences like universities. Mart is the word you imagine. Mart = mass merchandise + art distribution circuits.

What informs you and causes you to long for something beyond these encounters? While moving through these multiple terrains, you examine your sensations, feelings, and thoughts. You wonder what gives you pleasure. Is pleasure an important factor in life? It's difficult to remember when you are in the above-mentioned places. Are there new pleasures? Must one learn these? You wonder about the meaning of distinction. Can this have a meaning beyond referencing a market index? Does it relate to pleasure? Your dream continues.

As you move through the different buildings designated for display, questions come into your mind as you look and listen. An overall sensation of dimness and humidity is present. Lights are low, there are walls the color of melon. The primary impressions are that light, color, paper, textiles, and shapes exist. You are primarily sensitized to moving images, yet the systems of arrangement and interconnection between screens and space are what hold your attention. What you notice is a curved room with multiple screens displaying different intensities of green, people, details, and strategies that, in concert, form a broadcast sporting event. The other configuration you recall also involved multiple screens placed in a series of desks in the thoroughfare of the Halle. Your attention was caught by a performed monologue spoken with urgency about illegal confinement.

Questions form as you traverse the spaces: what can reach/touch us? Can we feel and think? Must we be bound and roped to feel? What is "we," "us," "I," or "you" any longer? What is the significance of any of these observations? How do processes, conditions, or things in these spaces matter? Beyond what is to be done, what can matter? What basis is there for understanding beyond the lowest common denominator, i.e., we are alive?

Upon awakening, you finger the documents confirming that you were in Kassel. You notice a creepy tinge of mild irritation as you see images on the pages you flip through. Why that sensation? What did you desire? Your mind wanders back to the word "distinction," and while wondering how anything can endure beyond a moment, you think of these words:

> Everything new is lost in something else new. Every illusion of being original disappears. The soul is cast down and turns its thoughts, with pain, albeit mixed with irony and a profound compassion, to those millions of feathered creatures, those innumerable agents of the mind, each of whom appears to himself to be the man (sic) of the moment, a free creator, the first mover, the possessor of an irrefragable certainty, a unique, distinctive source; and he who has spent his days in toil and who has used up his best moments in preserving his distinctiveness finds himself annihilated by the multitudes and swallowed up in the ever-growing swarms of those like himself.[2]

When returning to your embeddedly militarized metropolis, you find in a museum library, a magazine from another place and time. This description catches your attention, and you feel a mildly pleasurable sensation of recognition, but remind yourself that these sentiments are limited and considered obsolete. "There is no telling what the next Kassel Documenta would be. The thought is much too grim, and if we are to go by this year's Documenta..."[3]

1 "Why Reply?" is the title of a text preliminarily presented during the French journal *Multitudes* workshop at Documenta 12's Magazines Project. The workshop took place in Kassel, from June 26 to June 28, 2007. Other presenters were Maurizio Lazzarato, Yann Moulier Boutang, Éric Alliez, Gionvanna Zapperi, Brian Holmes, and Societé Realiste. A "counter-documenta" website was launched.

2 Paul Valéry, "Remerciement à l'académie française," in *Paul Valéry, Oeuvres*, Jean Hytier, ed., (Paris: Pléade, 1971), vol. 1, 731; note from Walter Benjamin, "Paul Valéry," in *Walter Benjamin: Selected Writings, 1931–1934*, Rodney Livingstone et al., trans.; Michael W. Jennings, Howard Eiland, and Gary Smith, eds. (Cambridge, MA: Belknap Press; Harvard University Press, 1999–2005), vol. 2, part 2, 532.

3 Serge Durant, "The Third Kassel Documenta," *Signals* 1, vol. 2 (September 1964), 7.

Aspen Art Museum Staff

Executive
Heidi Zuckerman
Nancy and Bob Magoon CEO and Director

Kristin Vemo
Executive Assistant to the Director

Curatorial
Courtenay Finn
Senior Curator

Lauren Fulton
Curatorial Associate and Rights & Reproduction Manager

Jonathan Hagman
Installation Director

Luis Yllanes
Chief Operating Officer

Jackie Zorn
Registrar

Installation Crew and Art Preparators
Seth Beckton
John Cohorst
Jason Cook
Vanessa Corona
Garrett Edquist
Takeo Hiromitsu
Ryan Jervis
Jason Mehl
Natalia Mills
Jason Smith
Dusty Spence

Design and Editorial
Edward Park
Graphic Design Intern

Sarah Stephenson
Editor

David Wise
Graphic Designer

Communications
Kelly Nosari
Public Relations and Marketing Manager

Development
Lisa DeLosso
Chief Development Officer

Melissa Jackson
Special Events Director

Kelsey Nemirov
Development Assistant

Abigail Reilly
Development Officer

Gerard Sonnier
Special Events Coordinator

Education
Michelle Dezember
Chief Program Officer

Annie Henninger
Access and Education Program Manager

Educators
Teresa Booth Brown
Kayla Hart
Chelsea Richards
Laci Wright

Finance and Administration
Janelle Caudill
Accounting Clerk

Lindy Clark
Human Resources Manager

Jenna Hasbrouck
Receptionist and Administrative Assistant

Karen Johnsen
Chief Financial Officer

Security and Visitor Information
Tiffany Lippincott
Guide Manager

Gregg Yocom
Security Director

Security Officers
Manny Doron
Bret Hitchcock
Mark Louderback
Jonathan Mackiewicz

Guides
Edward Barber
Zach Carver
Lynne Dyson
Ian Edquist
Kayla Hart
Daniel Hilbert
Rodney Hill
Katherine Marquez
Daniel Martinez
Dianna Platero
Chelsea Richards
Carly Rosenthal
Sue Shufro
Meg Thompson
Ines Vergara

Café
Mary Daly
Café Manager

Allen Domingos
Culinary Partner

Julia Domingos
Culinary Partner

Café Service Associates
Erin Erickson
Jordan Fox
Phoebe Fry
Talita Santos
Kristina Ugenti

Building and Facilities
Vince Hart
Facilities Assistant

Brian McKenna
Facilities Director

Shop
Shenna Richardson
Retail Manager

Shop Associates
Amy Dauer
Erin Erickson
Charlotte Hess
Roxy Montoya

Published by Aspen Art Press

Aspen Art Museum
637 East Hyman Avenue
Aspen, CO 81611
United States
aspenartmuseum.org

Library of Congress Control Number: 2016945091

ISBN: 978-0-934324-84-7

AAM exhibitions are made possible by the Marx Exhibition Fund. General exhibition support is provided by the Toby Devan Lewis Visiting Artist Fund.

AAM exhibitions are funded in part by the AAM National Council.

AAM education programs are made possible by the Questrom Education Fund. AAM talks and lectures are presented as part of the Questrom Lecture Series and made possible by the Questrom Education Fund.

Support for this publication is provided by the Toby Devan Lewis Publications Fund.

Reprints:
Heidi Zuckerman, "Pay Attention Mother Fuckers," in *Now You See It* (Aspen Art Press, 2008), 6–11.

Douglas Fogle, "On the Road with Catherine Opie," excerpted from *Catherine Opie: Skyways & Icehouses*, (Minneapolis: Walker Art Center, 2002), 4–7.

David Foster Wallace, "This is Water," Transcript of Kenyon Commencement Speech, 2005. © 2009, David Foster Wallace Literary Trust. Used with permission.

George Baker, "Paul Thek: Notes from the Underground," excerpted from *Paul Thek: Diver, A Retrospective*, eds. Elizabeth Sussman and Lynn Zelavansky (New York: Whitney Museum of American Art, 2010), 190–91.

Isa Genzken, "Two Exercises," in *Interfunktionen: Zeitschrift für Neue Arbeiten und Vorstellungen*, No. 11, Cologne, 1974. © 2018 Artist Rights Society (ARS), New York / VG Bild-Kunst, Bonn. Translation: Michael Robinson.

Hélio Oiticica, "Nitro Benzol & Black Linoleum," excerpted from *Hélio Oiticica: Quasi-Cinemas*, ed. Carlos Basualdo (Columbus: Wexner Center for the Arts, 2001), 81–9.

Heidi Zuckerman & Lynda Benglis, "You Can't Change Anything," excerpted from *Conversations with Artists* (Aspen Art Press, 2017), 35–41.

J.G. Ballard, "Dream Cargoes," *Shincho*, September 1990. © 1990 J.G. Ballard. Used by permission of The Wylie Agency LLC.

Renée Green, "Now It Seems Like A Dream," in *Other Planes of There* (Durham: Duke University Press, 2007), 408–10. © 2014 Duke University Press. All rights reserved. Republished by permission of the copyright holder.

Nancy and Bob Magoon CEO and Director
Heidi Zuckerman

Senior Curator
Courtenay Finn

Curatorial Associate and Rights & Reproduction Manager
Lauren Fulton

Editor
Sarah Stephenson

Graphic Designer
David Wise

Printing
The Prolific Group, Winnipeg, Canada

Typeface
Aspen Perennial by Radim Peško

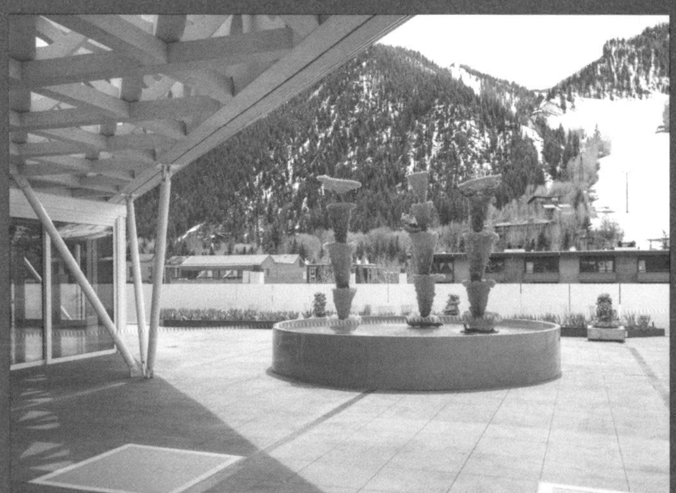

Cover
Installation view: Lynda Benglis, 2016. Aspen Art Museum.
Photo: Tony Prikryl

Aspen Art Museum
Aspen Art Museum
Aspen Art Museum
Aspen Art Museum